Praise for *The T*

The Teachers of Oz is a book that I read through cover to cover in one sitting because of the powerful messages told through emotional storytelling. The way Nathan and Herbie bring out challenging ideas and opportunities in education through the connection to *The Wonderful Wizard of Oz* did all the things that I hope for when reading any book; it made me laugh, cry, and think. As they reminded me in their book, teaching is a gift, and so is this book. I highly recommend this book for any educator.

> **—George Couros** (@gcouros), innovative teaching, learning, and leadership consultant, speaker, and author of *The Innovator's Mindset* and *Innovate Inside the Box*

The Teachers of Oz takes readers on a magnificent journey full of whimsy, nostalgia, and reflection. Written from the heart and based on experience and expertise in the field, Nathan and Herbie guide educators down the "yellow brick road," encouraging us to make connections, challenge assumptions, and land back on purpose—all while helping us to remember why we entered into this wonderful profession of education! A great addition to any educator's bookshelf!

> **—Dr. Jennifer Williams** (@JenWilliamsEdu), professor, education activist, author of *Teach Boldly*

Reading this book was like being invited to Nathan and Herbie's Maine home for inspiration, soul-searching, and professional balm. From learning about the villain, Mrs. Fridge-Box (you must read to find out about her!), to the lights and sounds of the Disneyland Christmas Parade, to the evolution of the buttonhole, this professional book is a brilliant allusion to *The Wonderful Wizard of Oz* and also weaves in beautiful story-telling. By traveling through Oz, we learn concrete strategies to embrace the type of teaching and learning that will light a fire beneath us! And the magic of the strategies is this: everything we need to become the teacher we always wanted to be is already inside of us. The book reminds us, "Teaching is a gift. It's not some prize to be achieved or some profession to find success in, but a gift to be completely realized, nurtured, and protected. That gift, that spark, is already there; this is the true self you must realize."

—Katie Novak, Ed.D. (@KatieNovakUDL), educational consultant, author of *UDL Now*, *UDL in the Cloud*, *Universally Designed Leadership*, and *Let Them Thrive*

The Teachers of Oz

THE
TEACHERS
OF OZ

Leading with Wisdom, Heart,
Courage, and Spirit

Herbie Raad and Dr. Nathan Lang-Raad

This book is available at special discounts when purchased in quantity for educational purposes or as premiums, promotions, or fundraisers. For inquiries and details, contact the publisher at books@daveburgessconsulting.com.

Published by Dave Burgess Consulting, Inc.
San Diego, CA
DaveBurgessConsulting.com

Illustrations by W. W. Denslow from *The Wonderful Wizard of Oz* (New York, 1900).

Library of Congress Control Number: 2020940149
Paperback ISBN: 978-1-951600-32-7
Ebook ISBN: 978-1-951600-33-4

Cover design by Michael Miller
Interior design by Liz Schreiter
Editing and production by Reading List Editorial: readinglisteditorial.com

CONTENTS

INTRODUCTION

❧

"If we walk far enough," said Dorothy, "I am sure we shall
sometime come to some place."

—L. Frank Baum, *The Wonderful Wizard of Oz*

Think back to the first time a student asked you a question you didn't know the answer to. Not just one of those answers that's easy to rattle off that you blanked on, but one you thought you *should* have known. What did you do? If you're like many people, you probably felt embarrassed and scrambled to sound like you knew what you were talking about, getting most of the pieces right, and then, once the day was saved, you googled the question later from the safety of a dark room. Why couldn't you simply have said, "You know what? I don't know, but let's find out together"?

The answer is simple yet challenging for our egos to hear. In our culture, if we don't know something, we feel we are perceived as not smart enough, not confident enough, or not engaged enough. Our culture thrives, and bases its sense of self-worth, on not only being right and having innate, effortless intelligence but being able to summon genius-level encyclopedic responses at all times without ever seeming to break a sweat. Teachers are viewed as authority figures and therefore viewed as having all of the answers. Sometimes we pretend to know lots of things we don't because the last thing we want to do is to appear unknowledgeable in front of our students or somehow lacking in front of our peers. We know the general limits of our own knowledge and, if cornered, keep those boundaries under wraps. We tell our students, "It's okay to fail," and "Embrace failure, learn from it," but we're not always willing to be transparent about our own areas of inexperience or what we just plain don't know.

In the fifth century BC, long before the machinery of academics, teaching, and learning operated as we know it today, Socrates said, "I know one thing, and that is that I know nothing." But somewhere along the meandering path of the education system's evolution, thanks in part to the introduction of standardization and the rise of the Internet, we teachers seem to have developed an obsession with looking authoritative, which has blinded us to the merits of embracing the unknown in education. Yet if we look at all of the inventions and innovations, and the enduring legacies of scholars both past and present, it is the unanswered questions that make learning—and life—fun and intriguing. After all, nothing would be known if we never took our first steps onto the road of the unknown.

How can we help our students embrace the journey into the unknown? *The Wonderful Wizard of Oz* has been a story that has resonated with us since as early as we can remember. Heartwarming and inspiring, it has enchanted audiences all over the world with its endearing characters and timeless life lessons since the original story was published in 1900. In 1939, the classic MGM film adaptation was produced, and an entirely new generation was introduced to the timeless magic of Baum's original story.

We have both loved the stories of Oz for our own reasons—Nathan because the characters were so interesting and intriguing, and Herbie because of the magic and the fun. But what is it about this book that keeps drawing us both back? And suddenly we realized—this is a story about a journey into the unknown. And each character has something different to tell us about what we all need for that journey—that the journey never ends. We would then further discover just how much the story helps us reconceptualize teaching. We've observed that the teachers who have the most success in their classrooms don't get mired down in the facts, i.e. the barrage of learning standards, lesson planning, etc. It's not that these teachers don't find these elements useful, but rather that they don't see them as an end in themselves. Successful teachers don't aim for the standards as a finish line—they begin there, just beyond them, right at the end of "The Student Will . . ." statement. Positive classroom experiences are created by a process: namely that of defined autonomy, where the focus is on the map of questions the standards elicit.

For over a century, the magical stories that unfold in L. Frank Baum's *The Wonderful Wizard of Oz* have captured our imaginations. In the classic children's novel, each of the four main characters sets out on a journey to answer their most deep-seated questions. As they travel down the yellow brick road to an expected happy ending, where the great and mysterious Wizard will grant their hearts' desires, they not only discover that they didn't know just how much they didn't know, they also learn perhaps the most important lesson of all—that the journey never ends.

Every journey is filled with innumerable twists and turns, obstacles and opportunities, good witches and wicked. Life isn't linear. In contrast, the way we organize teaching (grade levels, subjects, standards, etc.) contradicts this basic tenet and mistakenly teaches our students that life is linear: that you go from grade to grade, passing test after test, learning to demonstrate a list of competencies, in one linear trajectory, as if your existence progresses in an ordered, structured way to bring you to graduation. Only then do students enter the workforce and find that the real world is nothing like the classroom.

But in the Land of Oz, Dorothy finds that her new surroundings are quite different from the dusty, monotone Kansas she has only ever known (a linear and ordered world), but through her embrace of the journey, her new adventures, and her friendships, she discovers a new confidence to problem-solve, to trust herself to make sound judgments, to spread kindness and compassion, to explore the unknown with courage, and to lead others through a stronger and more balanced sense of self.

Drawing inspiration from the unforgettable characters and lessons of *Oz*, we've written *The Teachers of Oz* to help educators discover and leverage the attributes they seek most passionately. We hope to inspire teachers by tapping into familiar scenes and old friends—both good and wicked—from the Land of Oz to provision teachers with new tools, to reignite the fun, engaging, and meaningful learning environment both students (and teachers) crave. We'll also encourage you to seek out success on your own professional journey beyond the long and winding road of rosters, semesters, meetings, conferences, parents, and principals.

Each of the four primary characters in the original story is on a quest for a specific personal quality they believe they lack. Of course, by the time the Wicked Witch has been "liquidated," and the story has arrived at the end of the yellow brick road, we, as the audience, learn what we suspected all along: that the four friends already had exactly what they were searching for. Like so many of us, Dorothy, the Scarecrow, the Tin Man, and the Cowardly Lion couldn't see the amazing gifts they already possessed. The four friends had to embark on an epic journey filled with strife and adventure, conflict and resolution to see themselves clearly and discover that they indeed had those special qualities to begin with. Many education books available provide tips, tricks, templates, and strategies, all with the singular goal of equipping teachers and helping education professionals feel more effective. Although these tools are very helpful, we believe that all teachers can become more successful with a better sense of self, a deeper connection to traits they *already* possess (traits that, indeed, we *all* possess), and guidance about how to develop those traits even further. In this book, we'll discover that we have the brains, heart, courage, spirit, and leadership needed to face challenges and opportunities, collaborate effectively, and find our true selves in the midst of assumptions and illusions inside of education. This discovery is meant to transform the teaching experience, and therefore transform the learning experience for students.

"Come along, Toto," she said. "We will go
to the Emerald City and ask the Great Oz
how to get back to Kansas again."

—L. Frank Baum,
The Wonderful Wizard of Oz

1

Challenges in Education: We May Not Be in Kansas Anymore . . .

We have all, at one time or another, heard the phrase "We're not in Kansas anymore" to refer to a place or situation that's different from home—a departure from the comfortable and the familiar. For over a hundred years, the stories of the wonderful, magical Land of Oz have captured our imaginations. But, in the beginning, long before we learn to fear the evil plotting of the Wicked Witch or want to help a cowardly lion to find his courage, a young girl named Dorothy, accustomed to a life of monochrome monotony, utters these words as she takes her first steps into a brand-new world far from the only home she has ever known (thanks to a rather convenient cyclone).

For the most part, we in education remain stuck in our own version of Kansas. It's true that school reform has been in the making for years and many of us are pursuing the change we want to see by working long hours to help our students succeed. We've made great strides, and there are indeed pockets of magic and creativity in classrooms across the nation. But sadly, this just isn't the norm. Excitement and passion are not the standard.

Teachers are told they must adhere to a rigid system they were never allowed to help build. Teachers tell students what they will learn (targets and objectives), how they will learn (endless practice problems; copying notes from yet another lecture; a "Story of the Week" with a detailed reading log; and worksheets so ponderous and endless that they strip all relevant value and interest from their original lesson goal), where they will learn it (sitting at their desks that rarely move, anchored just as intractably as their classrooms), and all for the goal of passing a test, so that they may move on to another test, advancing to the next grade level, the next school, and yet another empty box to mark "Done." We cannot allow our classrooms to continue this way.

True learning begins when students feel like they're a part of something personally meaningful in the classroom, when they're in a space that inspires them to follow their curiosity, to embrace wonder and discovery. We have come to a crossroads. Our world demands that education cannot stay in Kansas any longer. There's a cyclone of change looming darkly on the horizon. It is up to all of us to embrace and encourage that change. As teachers, we face many challenges, many influences that want to keep us in Kansas, that want us to uphold the status quo at any cost. How do we lead the change of learning in the classroom and become champions of something truly authentic and transformative? To truly serve our students and prepare them for the future, we must:

1. Give students freedom to express their own creativity and choose what, how, when, and where they learn.
2. Inspire students to wonder and care more, so that they naturally expand their own thinking.
3. Coach and support student learning ardently.
4. Create a classroom community that embraces different points of view and promotes outlandish ideas, allowing students the

flexibility to change their minds, and to fail in a safe, supportive environment while gaining the confidence and ability to overcome challenges.

Freedom

Schooling can sometimes feel as though it's more about generating good little cogs in a meaningless system of endless predictability than it is about creating avenues for students to use their own voices, creativity, and talents. Being a part of a classroom should be and can be energizing—an experience that inspires us to learn and be creative. But this can happen only if the time spent in school (both inside and outside the classroom) is fun and meaningful and connects to students' own interests and choices; it can't happen simply through forced compliance and obligation. Classrooms must represent freedom—freedom granted to students to speak their minds and freedom to seek help and advice from those peers or adults they trust. The purest form of learning happens when it is sought out, when it is a voluntary decision to answer the question "Why?" When students are connecting with others who have similar interests—whether in person or via texts, media, or independent solitary musings—they collaborate, share ideas, and question each other.

When Dorothy first lands in Oz, she arrives in the midst of a civil war of sorts. The Wicked Witch of the East had "held all the Munchkins in bondage for many years, making them slave for her night and day." How many of us have experienced, firsthand, or at least known *that* teacher, whose classroom-management style is similarly tyrannical? The teacher who might be so close to retirement that they have checked out. Or the teacher who's been overworked to the point of burnout. And of course, in some cases, there's the teacher who simply does not like their job.

Finding Freedom: Herbie's Experience

I had a life-changing moment in the third grade. To minimize my presence as a distraction in class, my teacher brought in a cardboard refrigerator box and erected it around my desk so that I was completely cut off from the rest of the class. Now, it should be said, with a nod to fairness, that I was (and might still be, if you ask Nathan on the right day) quite a handful. I was hyperactive, constantly questioning, and the perennial class clown who would do anything to make my class-mates giggle. My teacher, Mrs. Fridge-Box, as we'll call her to protect her anonymity, had tried any number of solutions to subdue and pun-ish her most trying student: sending me to sit outside alone on the con-crete, holding me back from learning my multiplication tables (which I loved, and at which I excelled), trotting me off to see the principal, holding parent conferences, and far too many other strategies to list here, lest this story become as frustrated and tired as Mrs. Fridge-Box had most assuredly become.

I distinctly remember the embarrassment and humiliation, delib-erately engineered by Mrs. F-B, as she threw me even further into the spotlight by erecting four walls around me to smother my natural enthusiasm. But do not worry. I remember the embarrassment and humiliation lasting exactly five minutes.

The machinations of Mrs. F-B backfired on her most spectacu-larly when I remembered what all young students remember when they have a moment to themselves—to have fun. During recess, I was forced to stay behind in the classroom, and when Mrs. Fridge-Box left the room, I grabbed some crayons and set to work on my very first DIY home improvement project. I drew a doorknob, a window, and some pretty flowers and grass on the outer walls of my new box home, turning it into my own little house. From the comfort of my new for-tress, I was free to put on puppet shows for the other students, sing my favorite songs at the top of my little lungs whenever I wanted to, or even stand on my desk on my tiptoes—peeking over the top of my box—whenever I had a question which, alas, was often.

Needless to say, Mrs. F-B very sadly lost her temper again. (My mother was also less than pleased to hear about the Great Boxing, which, after a call to the principal, disappeared the following morning.) But I do remember in that moment learning just how much power I had and how I could now use it against my archnemesis whenever it tickled me, which is of course exactly what I did until summer vacation. Incidentally, Mrs. Fridge-Box retired after that school year, never to be seen again.

The moral of our tale? You can try to put your problems in a box, but they will always find a way out again; or, also: students need freedom and the structure to grow into who they will eventually become. In retrospect, it's clear what I was doing *was* learning, just on my own schedule, and in my own way. I was independently, if unknowingly, taking my first steps onto the road toward my passion for creative artistry and my future in the performing arts. Had Mrs. F-B been able to channel my gifts rather than try to stifle them, both of us would now have vastly different memories of that long-ago third grade classroom. Mrs. Fridge-Box might have offered me an opportunity to learn in different ways. She could have allowed me to create a story, song, or play based on the text I was reading or math problems we were solving. She could have allowed me to work independently and supported me rather than trying to fit me into the quite literal box she thought I *should* occupy.

Thus endeth the lesson.

When you're a part of a classroom that embraces empowerment and freedom, it's not governed by initiatives, mandates, rules, or "boxes." Students draw from a wellspring of energy fueled by unfiltered autonomy, transparency, connection, and generosity. If you are able to tap into your students' gifts, there is no limit to what students and teachers may achieve.

Motivation: Wondering and Caring More

How do we motivate students? How do we, as their teachers and guides, inspire them to wonder and care? There is a direct correlation between what we think and wonder about, and the intrinsic care we are then able to feel. How *can* we engage students in a way that helps them develop their own thinking? Sometimes called "the silver bullet" of the education world—and of life, in general—how is the fire of *interest* first ignited?

As the planet spins faster and faster, we have all the secrets of the universe at our fingertips at all times. Falling down the rabbit hole of a Google search has never been easier. How, then, living inside the depthless realm of instant and fascinating distraction, can we introduce another option, a different road . . . one that leads to more organized learning, lasting comprehension, and, most importantly, a way to make our students *care*?

The secret of all engaged participation lies in the hidden and simple power of *relatability*. Dorothy's entire time in the Land of Oz, once the cyclone crash-lands her there, is spent with one simple goal in mind: to go home again. In one blazing moment of clarity, she knows exactly what she wants, and she takes us along with her as she tries to find her way.

Every friend she makes learns about her seemingly impossible problem and stands by her side to lend whatever help they can give. And we, as the observers, all want to help her, too. We are able to relate to her fear and distress at the prospect of never seeing her family ever again.

With the dazzling flurry of tech, and the immediacy of social media, how can we help our students relate to—and care about—the material they need to learn? The best way is to get them to tell their own stories. Storytelling is a powerful way for students to share their thinking. It is instantly engaging and intrinsically motivating. A great storyteller helps us decide not only what is compelling in life, but why it's compelling. A great storyteller ascends Bloom's taxonomy by displaying all levels of cognitive processing, from recalling information to creating new experiences. Through sensory detail, figurative language, and the call to action, the storyteller helps us interpret information, make new and meaningful connections, and reconstruct that information as part of a new and different creation, namely our reflections on those stories.

A great story, then, is not about the regurgitation of facts, though it can most definitely inform. It's also not only about the storyteller, though it most certainly transforms their experience of an event when telling it. A great story invites the listener to expand their mind and think differently about the world. It also positions the storyteller to influence the listener or reader so that they reevaluate their opinions, thoughts, beliefs, and actions.

Here's a story to illustrate the point about why stories matter. After we moved to Maine, we decided to become gardeners. But long before we could pick our own vegetables and flowers, we had to start somewhere. So we began researching how to create a vegetable garden (after all, now that we're here in Maine, we expect to see Martha Stewart around every corner, or at least we hope for that). Combing through websites on how to garden in our growing zone and watching Martha Stewart episodes (literally every single one) represented the information stage.

The next stage was the application of that new knowledge, the actual process of tilling the ground, fertilizing the soil, buying the seeds, and sowing them indoors before planting outdoors during Memorial Day weekend. We could have simply opted to rush out and build a garden based on our limited prior experiences and knowledge of gardening, but it wouldn't necessarily have led to any success. So instead, we informed ourselves before we acted. We metaphorically and literally started from the ground up, and now we have a vibrant garden that produces vegetables to harvest, beautiful roses for our home, as well as all the knowledge we've gained and the fun adventures we've had along the way.

Once we created our garden, it was wisdom we gained from experience that not only allows us to maintain the garden but helped us design a garden that also self-sows and flourishes. Wisdom protects it from the early autumn freeze in October that whispers with its frosts of the snows that are soon to fall. Wisdom helps us learn more about our property's optimal locations for soil and sunlight. It allows us to learn what insects and animals will try to eat our crops and ways to mitigate their endless appetites. But it is not only wisdom. It is wonder and it is care. We have a personal, emotional, and financial investment in this garden.

A great storyteller is like the gardener who not only creates beautiful gardens with bountiful crops but who has the courage to create a variety of other kinds of gardens, and maybe builds a greenhouse, and teaches others how also to build and maintain their own gardens. Storytelling creates skill beyond just the telling of stories—it teaches students how to relate to each other, to empathize, how to inform, entertain, and connect to people who are different from them.

Ursula K. Le Guin once said, "Science describes accurately from outside, poetry describes accurately from inside. Science explicates, poetry implicates. Both celebrate what they describe." Storytelling is a conduit between science and poetry. It allows us to celebrate both "languages" as tools to speak about the objective through our unique subjective lens. For students, storytelling is more than just a regurgitation of events. It's painting a picture having the materials in mind (elements of the story) and also the final work of art (perception created).

A great storyteller has an appreciation of the information that's available but digs deeper to find the true meaning behind the facts, takes action on the new information, transforms their thinking, and tells the story in such a way that it shapes the way others think.

Students learn to wonder and care when they learn how to tell stories at this deeper level. Teachers can explicitly teach storytelling to their students by asking students to share their thinking. When a student tells a story from their own perspective, they are expressing their understanding on an intellectual level as well as revealing in detail how they think and feel about a particular experience or concept. When student thinking is effectively shared and heard, teachers and fellow students are equipped with the information needed to join in on the student's perspective. Feedback from teachers supports students in providing powerful language metaphors and confidence in expressing their unique voice.

Becoming a Coach

Because, as K–12 educators, we are adults and our students are children, we might believe that our communication must be direct and one directional. This reflects a very Industrial Age mentality and does not lead to empowering students. In education, we often impose a carrot-on-a-stick system of rules and compliance. This punishment-and-reward structure can cause a student to pretend to be someone they're not because they don't want to be rejected or marginalized by the teacher or their peers. This kind of unhealthy learning environment encourages students to do only those things they believe would be favorably received by the teacher or the "good kids in class." In a sense, they mimic the most influential figure in the room: the teacher. Students feel like they must wear a mask, say what they think the teacher wants to hear, and keep others from getting to know who they really are. Or they might just tune out or drop out altogether.

Thankfully, empowering and supportive language is contagious, and we can weave it into the very fabric of the classroom by using coaching instead of a traditional teaching model. With a coaching approach, the teacher's attention is on the students, and the focus is squarely on those learning outcomes that have been established for them. It's not a show or performance, and there is no one to impress—there is just unbridled student energy emerging out from a fountain of support. This model of teaching is effective if it's employed purposefully and positively on students' aspirations and when it clearly connects their actions (interests, work ethic, collaboration, perseverance, etc.) to the learning outcomes (effect, performance, growth goals, etc.). Educators must provide students with the recognition, affirmation, praise, and feedback they not only deserve but need.

This is evident in classrooms where you see students showing leadership and taking ownership of their learning. The conversations are focused on the task at hand and are led by the student. Instead of the teacher asking all the questions, students must generate questions and conversation. The teacher guides from the periphery of the conversation and helps students clarify one another's thinking. Student questions should revolve around the "why," justifying and contrasting the strategies used, and not just center around "What answer did you get?" Being a leader means the way students think is important; therefore, student conversations should go beyond providing answers when asked.

Community

As educators, most of us believe (and research confirms) that our students learn through discovery, creativity, innovation, and problem-solving. The future of our educational system and the vitality of our economy depend on it. We often attempt to create this environment through scalable and systematic initiatives like backward mapping or unit planning. Although these are important tasks for effective planning, will these strategies lead to our students becoming critical thinkers, innovators, and creators?

Educators often use the word *community* to describe the structure we work in while collaborating (like a Professional Learning

Community). There's also the *school community*, with its many "stake-holders." But it's even more important to develop a community in the classroom, to support teachers and give students the permission to create, think critically, and amplify their voices, so they become the leaders of the present and future.

A *classroom community* isn't just an afterthought. Created conscientiously, it can provide the energy and foundation to inspire students to create and share their voices. Instead of providing a static curriculum, a classroom community supports students as they create content and share their gifts freely within that community. Instead of grades, a classroom community provides feedback to help students strengthen communication skills. Instead of telling students to complete worksheets or tasks, students within a classroom community can spark one another's entrepreneurial spirit by providing opportunities to use resources (people and tools) to make a difference in the world. A community offers opportunities for students to engage in projects that are interesting to them and that have a strong, relevant connection to their daily lives and the community they live in.

Today's problems are too complex to be solved by a conventional classroom mired in the practices of the past. Innovative problem-solving hinges entirely on forward thinking; therefore, we must actively apply strategies, knowledge, and skills learned from each other. A collaborative, transparent community illuminates and encourages students. Imagine the wisdom we could attain and the learning transformation that could occur with effective collaboration in a supportive classroom community.

Even if we realize we can no longer remain in "Kansas," that we're on the road toward more freedom, coaching, and community in the classroom, why is it still so difficult for us to change? Why have we settled for the education status quo for so many decades?

When navigating any change, we (as educators and as students) must remember that we all need time to adjust. We don't all simultaneously evolve and adapt without effort. When we're patient with the initial stages of discomfort and disorientation caused by change, we eventually find equilibrium again, and we experience the benefits we were too stressed to be aware of at first. When helping others navigate whether to stick with the status quo or adopt changes, we have to be able to articulate the importance of broadening the experiential horizon, to provide support (if wanted and asked for), and to provide a map of where the change may lead us. We also have to deploy a surplus of patience . . . because this particular trip down the road of yellow brick can indeed be a long and winding one.

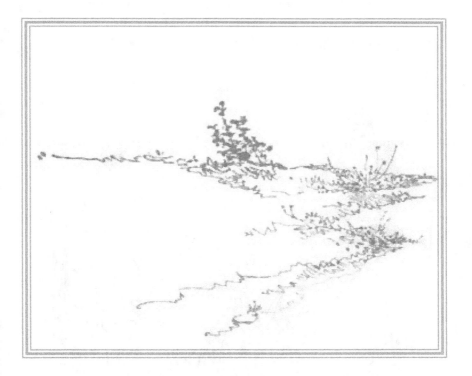

"Can't you give me brains?" asked the Scarecrow.

"You don't need them. You are learning something every day. A baby has brains, but it doesn't know much. Experience is the only thing that brings knowledge, and the longer you are on earth the more experience you are sure to get."

—L. Frank Baum,
The Wonderful Wizard of Oz

2

Wisdom: Scarecrow

Scarecrow thinks he doesn't have a brain. When we first meet him in his cornfield, he humbly confesses that his head is filled only with straw. Even though he doubts himself, he demonstrates consistently that not only is he capable of deep reasoning, but that he already has the brains he seeks, displaying high levels of problem-solving, wisdom, and common sense.

When Dorothy cannot find a way to lower him down and free him from his pole in the cornfield, it is the Scarecrow who comes up with the solution for his own liberation. Later in the story, when the friends stumble across an orchard of apple trees (who, as it turns out, happen to be less than enthusiastic to part with their apples), it is the Scarecrow who figures out that redirecting the trees' anger back against them will, successfully, yield free airborne apples. Time and again, it is the Scarecrow's innate ability to coolly think through obstacles that helps his friends—and ultimately the Scarecrow himself—surmount all odds.

In the novel, it is revealed that he is only two days old and therefore hasn't acquired the experience needed to build knowledge. As teachers, we understand that we can't know every instructional strategy or every facet of the content we teach. Even though we understand this, do we apply it? In this chapter, we will look at how to glean the most from your experience, make learning more authentic, discover what we value most about learning, and appreciate the contributions we make in real time in an education landscape filled with constantly changing pressures and demands.

Authentic Learning

Scarecrow, who wanted to experience the world in a very authentic and specific way, can serve as an excellent model for educators looking for ways to give students more experiences and to transform the classroom into a more authentic space. Authentic learning happens when students are engaged in learning that is both meaningful to them and, by mirroring the world outside the classroom, relatable in a way that encourages cascading retention rather than blind memorization. Just as the enslaved flying monkeys of the Wicked Witch of the West blindly follow the commands of their evil mistress, students who are sentenced to vapid memorization of lists, tables, and facts find their skills reduced to the singular and narrow experience of temporary recall rather than authentic learning.

Authentic learning is important because it inspires students. It has a direct impact on their daily lives and encourages them to take action in their school community and to make an impact on the world. Authentic experiences shouldn't be forced by asking students to build projects using pretend scenarios (you are a construction worker and you want to . . . , or you are a business owner and you want to . . .), or by incorporating themes kids simply don't care about. Imagine how motivated students would be if we stopped assigning *work* and instead provided opportunities to *create*, igniting an experience of pride and achievement. Imagine inspiring students to a level of creativity and individuality where a student, perhaps for the first time, finds their voice. That's the real magic of authentic learning: true, genuine, intrinsic inspiration, rather than an accidental byproduct of a homework assignment.

How can you create truly authentic learning experiences that are rich in content, deepen thinking and learning, but don't feel like "doing school"? These five questions can help support your approach to authentic learning:

1. How are you creating an environment that doesn't "feel like school"?
2. What do you intend for students to do with the new learning?
3. How will you create an experience that sparks intrinsic motivation driven by inquiry?
4. How will you create experiences that balance individuality with teamwork?
5. How will you help unleash your students' talents?

Build a Better Learning Environment

Let's admit that many classrooms, more often than not, still tend to be cluttered with desks, in unnatural, glaring fluorescent lighted spaces, with walls sprinkled with static posters that condescendingly dictate rather than inspire, and obligatory homework assignments written on whiteboards that can feel tyrannical rather than educational. We are constantly building and rebuilding our personal world (whether consciously or unconsciously) in certain ways which help us to feel good, which help us to feel strong and inspired. Why should the classroom be any different?

Sometimes, getting away from the paradigm of the traditional classroom or school building is the best way to foster authentic learning. Imagine if you were forced to live your entire life in the same room. How would you want it to look? What would make you the most comfortable, the most inspired? As creatures of habit, we sometimes turn a blind eye to the perfunctory surroundings we inherit, conditioning ourselves to accept a banal inevitability without realizing that even the smallest alteration can send ripples of change out into the world.

We can all imagine classrooms that mirror the outside world and provide space for our students to dream, design, and create. We *can* transform the prison into a palace of possibilities. Compelling, dynamic spaces expose us to new environments and ways of thinking that push convention, challenge the traditional, and allow us to see and feel things in unexpected ways.

We are not suggesting maxing out your credit card to furnish your classroom with the latest and greatest trends and designs, or installing elaborate media centers with the newest technology which become obsolete almost daily. But can you make small changes to elicit feelings of warmth, comfort, and fun, so that your students feel excited to see and experience the space every day? Teachers creating unique greetings for kids when they walk through their doors, organic laughter and smiles present, warm lamps instead of bright overhead lights, and the elimination of a teacher's desk are some examples of how to create this warmer, welcoming, more genuine (and generous) tone.

Create Relatable Learning Intentions

When we ask students, "What's something interesting you learned today?" students will often share an interesting fact they've just learned. However, when we go on to ask, "What does that mean to you?" or "What are you going to do with that new learning?" or "What does that inspire you to do?" we might get a shrug or confused look. Interesting phenomena and surprising information are helpful as hooks to coax students into new learning, but if students only remember the gimmick and don't make practical applications, they don't engage in deeper, complex learning about the concept. To fully master a concept, students need to be able to make connections to situations outside the classroom, predictable or unpredictable, and to ask, "Why and how does this apply to me?" To help our students master a concept, we must introduce the most secret of all secret ingredients (and perhaps the most elusive): relatable context.

For all two days of his young life, Scarecrow's world was defined entirely within the narrow boundaries of his cornfield, and the bullying crows he was powerless to fend off. It is through Dorothy's kindness and compassion that the Scarecrow is set free to step outside the safe and comfortable limits of his known world and set off on an adventure to self-discovery. Though she herself is new to Oz and still finding her bearings, Dorothy's brave and empathetic nature liberates the Scarecrow, opening up the way for him to explore the world.

Encourage Intrinsic Motivation Driven by Inquiry

When you see the word *inquiry*, you might imagine an activity that uses prompts to help students ask additional and better questions. Truly authentic experiences create intrinsic drives for students to ask more questions. These questions take the student to depths not previously predicted by the teacher. Intrinsically motivated questions are those students generate based on genuine interest in a subject. They give them further insight into how they and others see the world, and they take students to new, unanticipated depths. These questions might arise from students attempting to solve a problem and realizing they need more answers before they generate a solution. These are the kinds of questions that organically surface at home when parents are cooking: "Why does that bubble?" or "Why does that change colors?" One of the most important skills we can teach our students is how to ask the interesting and unheard-of questions. We can google anything today and get an answer. But authentic learning is about generating new questions.

Even though the Scarecrow was "born" in the magical Land of Oz, with its dizzying array of wonders, his original purpose is set firmly in stone—immutable and not to be altered—to remain within the limited confines of his cornfield, never to wander past the boundaries of his field. But as his corn grows, so too does Scarecrow's innate curiosity about the world around him. It is only when Dorothy asks him if he might like to accompany her on her way to the Emerald City to see the Wizard, that the Scarecrow first begins to explore the notion that his world might indeed be bigger than he first imagined. Had he been left alone forever, his natural curiosity would have continued to grow as time passed. It took Dorothy's singularly unique influence (like that of a teacher and a student) to give him the independence, encouragement, and freedom to flourish. When the sovereignty of freedom and independence to learn collides with curiosity and experience, the journey toward true wisdom begins.

Balance Individuality with Teamwork

When it comes time for students to enter the workforce, they may be required to work in teams—to *collaborate*. This is one reason we give when we group students together to work on challenges and projects, all in the righteous name of *collaboration*—which begs the eternal question: Is it better to be able to solve problems individually or by collaborating with others? To compound the issue of balanced group work and add chaos to cacophony, we may integrate the latest tech tools, to establish constant communication with their teacher and peers. New research by Harvard Business School professor Ethan Bernstein suggests that "always on" collaboration may not always be effective. Instead, "intermittently on" might be better for complex problem-solving. Instead of forcing students to be in constant collaboration, we can build the best environment when we provide a balance of group work with individual think time and reflection.

Of course, one size does not always fit all, and Common Sense needs to be able to wave her wand and rule the day. As throughout the Land of Oz, Glinda's kind and gentle wisdom is ever-present and watchful, always guiding without controlling, leading without dom-inating, so too should establishing the individual vs. collaborative structure belong to the teacher's experienced and intrinsically unique purview. Back in Oz, another example of this balance is found when our new friends have to make individual decisions about whether to travel with Dorothy to the land in the south. During the journey they end up working as a team, but each of the friends has to make indi-vidual decisions for themselves about whether or not they will join her. Certain students will most definitely respond more favorably to being able to problem-solve on their own, in their own space, and in their own time, while others will crave dynamic group interaction. Being able to distinguish between these two very disparate personality groups and gently granting them the freedom and appropriate space they need to grow is vital if one is to promote a safe, comfortable, and effective learning space. Ensure that students have space to work and reflect by themselves in a quiet place, or allow students to reflect in other places besides the whole-group classroom environment (e.g., a cozy place in the room). Additionally, ensure that those students who thrive in group settings have a structured time to talk out their learn-ing to others. A great time for this is morning meeting or closing circle for the day.

Unleash Your Students' Talents

Our primary focus as educators is to help students discover their pas-sion, purpose, and voice. Everyone has the capacity to impact the world, but we all need encouragement and support to help tap into our talents and strengths. Once students identify their strengths (teachers create the environment for this through consistent and regular affirmation), they gain the confidence to take action and lead. This cycle creates the momentum to learn and spread ideas. We can help students unleash their talents by not only affirming them, but by removing barriers that keep them from discovery. A part of removing barriers is establishing a feedback structure. It's crucial that teachers give timely feedback while students are solving problems, both in small groups and in individual conversations, and not just on a concluding assessment. This communication ensures students have time to react to, and implement, the feedback through revisions. The specific and understandable nature of feedback helps students know exactly what parts of their reasoning need revision and what parts of their solution path should be revisited. Avoid vague language and empty praise. Feedback must be actionable, kind, helpful, and clear.

Thought should be given to how feedback is delivered. Is it in daily conversation? If working in an online document, will the teacher provide comments in the document itself or in another creative platform? How often are academic or learning conferences held? Will feedback take precedence over grades? Will students be encouraged to reflect on feedback, and how? These are structures and expectations that a teacher would explicitly communicate to students.

Rules, policies, rigidity, tests, etc., keep students stuck in playing the game of school, jumping through hoops, and not seeing the connection between school and the world. Can we encourage our students' independence so that they will continue to be strong enough once they leave our classrooms to maintain their unique personalities and not lose themselves in the pursuit of success?

The Lesson of Determination: Herbie's Experience

In 1998, the night before Thanksgiving, I was given a gift that would change the course of my life. Always preferring my own company and shying away from any sort of public attention, it is perhaps ironic that I have been fortunate enough to make my living as a professional singer, where it is my job to perform in front of large crowds of people. At the age of ten, I was noticed by a talent scout who, hearing me sing in a small local performance, asked me to go to New York to appear in the title role of the Broadway revival of the musical *Oliver!* For all the Broadway-philes reading this, it was to be a major event starring Ron Moody as Fagin and Patti LuPone in the role of Nancy.

After all the calls and contract details had been deliberated, my mother (who, it was established, would have to chaperone me to the East Coast) and I were planning and packing excitedly when my father declared that I would not be going to New York. Codependent and controlling, he would not allow either of us to go, not for any other reason other than that he had "made his decision." When the talent agent offered to chaperone me, which would have allowed my mother to stay home in California, the answer from my father was still no. No son of his would be "prancing like a sissy" on stage while other people watched. And so, just like that, my Broadway debut was relegated to the land of What-Might-Have-Been.

Of course, like all irrational tyrants, my father's battle was a losing one. After all, you may cage the bird, but you cannot stop him from singing. And sing I did. For decades, my mother applauded in the front row while my father bristled, powerless at home, refusing to ever see me perform.

When I was twenty-five, even though I had been lucky enough to find steady work with my hometown theater company, the Santa Barbara Civic Light Opera, where I learned my craft working in every capacity both on stage and in the wings, I auditioned to be a Christmas caroler in the Disneyland Christmas Parade. It used to be that, at the end of the parade, singers would walk down Main Street in full festive winterwear singing Christmas carols for the guests. Anyone who has ever visited a Disney property knows that they just do everything right. They are able to create magic and memories like no other company on earth. No detail is ever left up to chance. Not even the audition process, as I would soon learn.

After my three-hour drive to Anaheim from Santa Barbara, I waited around with the hundreds of other hopefuls for hour after hour for my chance to get into the room and sing my song in front of the creative team. They were only allowing eight bars of music! (Normally, at auditions, you are allowed to sing sixteen bars, which is already a severely shortened version of your music.) Because they had to get through so many singers in one day, the casting department was forced to streamline the process. I was "called back" later that same day to learn and sing music that I would be taught by the Disney team. I made the cut and was asked to return the following day for another round of auditions in front of yet another panel of executives. After another grueling eight-hour day, I drove back home to Santa Barbara. Three back-to-back days of auditioning and interviews (and driving) followed, whereupon I returned home convinced that I had landed my first job at the Happiest Place on Earth.

The next day, after LIVING next to the phone and jumping out of my seat every time it rang, I was called by a Disney casting director, very politely thanked, and told that I was not what they were looking for. My heart broke as it only can when one is in their twenties. I thanked the casting director and said that, while I was saddened, I had enjoyed the process and couldn't wait to try out again the following year. I wondered later if this was part of the interview process because, as I was about to hang up, the casting director said that while I wasn't "right" for the parade, they were considering me for a role in a new show called *Animazement* that had just opened. She asked if I might be interested in being featured in it as "Aladdin" from their classic film. I mean . . . can you imagine? It was as if the Genie had emerged from the phone in an explosion of blue smoke to grant all my wishes!

Another round of auditions followed. I learned new music, was taught choreography, and was asked to improv in character. Round after round, I successfully passed the other auditioning candidates until I made it to the final phase where I had to pass muster for the Character Department. This was the most grueling test of all. It didn't matter that I sounded like the character. If the Character Department didn't think I *looked* like him, I was doomed. An Aladdin wig (with his trademark red fez) was put on my head and styled to my face. My eyebrows were darkened and shaped, and the team took Polaroids of my face from different angles.

Once again I drove home. Once again I waited by the phone, sure that my dream was about to come true. And, once again, the phone rang and I was told that I wasn't what they were looking for. Exhausted and more disappointed than I could ever remember feeling, I once again thanked the casting director and asked if I might audition again for the role. The response was that I probably shouldn't waste my time. She thanked me politely and hung up. Devastation.

In the category of: Never Give Up—I stalked the Disneyland casting hotline and advertisements in the entertainment trade papers for news of auditions for the show. I went to two more rounds of auditions for the same role in the same show. The audition process became more demanding. The show had proved popular with the guests, and now everyone in Los Angeles was auditioning for it. I knew I was right for it. I knew that I wanted it. But I also knew that all I could do was to do my best with every opportunity I was given.

After my third audition for the show, life moved on, and I went back to checking the Disneyland hotline for the next audition for *Animazement*. I needn't have worried, however, for the night before Thanksgiving, my mother had driven to pick me up from work at the Granada Theatre in Santa Barbara, where I had been working for the costume department backstage as a dresser. (My car had died from all that driving back and forth to Disneyland.) As I hopped in the front seat, she said that a casting director from Disneyland had just called the house that evening (this was before we all had iPhones) and said she would be calling again that night to speak with me. My mother had very wisely removed my father from the equation by having calls to the house phone forwarded to her cell phone. (She was always the first in our family to have the newest technology.) She had only just finished telling me about the call when her phone rang from a 714 number. We both screamed, and I picked up. I was offered the understudy position of Aladdin and asked if I would be able to start rehearsals in Anaheim in a few weeks. Success at last!

A month of rehearsals and Disney training followed. I would arrive early to the park, just to walk around, completely disbelieving that I was now a part of the famed Disney magic. I actually belonged here now! At night, when rehearsals finished for the day, I would walk along Main Street watching the lights twinkle in the trees, hearing the laughter of everyone around me, seeing Sleeping Beauty's castle in the distance, and feeling like the luckiest person in the world.

On my first day of rehearsal, my new cast was taken to watch the current cast perform the show. We were all so excited as it is not always the case in the performing world that one gets to see a show up and running prior to joining it. Afterward, we went backstage, where we got to meet our counterparts. I was shocked, though now in retrospect not very surprised, that the actor I was understudying behaved rather cold and distant to me and said, "Sorry, but you'll never be performing this role. I opened the show. I created this performance, and I never miss a day." Of course, I tried to be as polite as possible. I smiled, complimented his performance, and thought, "Well, at least I will enjoy it for as long as I can, and even if I never get to perform it, I'm still happier than that guy will ever be. I've gotten this far. Let's just have fun."

Well, we all sailed through the rehearsal process, and I returned home exhausted, but satisfied in a way that I had never been before. I resigned myself to the knowledge that I would probably never get to perform the show, until one month later when I got a call at seven a.m. from one of the stage managers. That same full-time Aladdin I had met backstage had called in sick. Could I make it from Santa Barbara to help them out and take over the role for the day? That one day of performances turned into a couple days a month, which quickly turned into a part-time spot during the summer when the park is in peak season and the show's performance schedule was increased to run seven days a week. Before the year was over, I had been offered the full-time position, replacing that same actor who had decided to quit!

We performed five thirty-minute shows per day, and during the next three years, until the show closed, I performed the role of Aladdin in *Animazement* more than any other actor—over 3,000 times!

The role for which I had been turned down multiple times, the position I had been repeatedly told I was not right for, became mine after all, and I have never forgotten the sheer joy of every single moment of it. There was never one single day from 1998 to 2001 when I didn't wake up excited and looking forward to going to work. I had never had that experience before. Sure, there were days when my body was tired and sore. Yes, there were days when I had more energy than others. (I once performed *fifty* shows over ten consecutive days.) But I promise you, there was not one single moment when I wasn't happy to the point of giddiness at the thought of what I was doing. I was aware, every single second, without exception, just how fortunate I was to be where I was and doing what I loved to do. *Animazement* was the equivalent of the college experience I'd always heard others enjoyed. I learned more in that period than in any other. I learned some very important lessons, not always in the easiest ways, but they are lessons I carry with me to this very day. The show closed as a direct result of 9/11, when the entertainment division across Disney properties was affected. But my days in the Happiest Place on Earth truly remain some of the happiest of my life, and I will never forget how grateful I felt, and feel, to have been given the great gift of being even a small part of such an amazing legacy of magic and work.

What Do We Value?

As educators, we can prepare students for the world by letting them experience failure so they can learn how to overcome it, just as Herbie did. As a matter of fact, we'd be wise to change our language around failure. We need to reframe the concept of "failure"; as an organic part of the learning process, we should stop using the term as it relates to learning. We can act on this mindset by allowing students multiple opportunities to refine and improve their work, and by encouraging them to never give up because they are too special and the world needs them. We must give them the freedom to make their own choices and help them cultivate their own happiness, whether what makes them happy is conducting science experiments in the kitchen or singing in their bedroom. Let's tell them what they're good at and celebrate their senses of humor. Learning doesn't result from rules and mandates, activities and tests, but from a shared commitment to doing work that is fun and that matters.

Learning in its truest and most powerful form transforms the common activities of the classroom into matters of lasting value, learning that transcends problems on a worksheet or textbook. Think about a learning standard that's deemed essential for your classroom. We believe it's essential because truly mastering that learning standard demonstrates an understanding of that aspect as it emerges from the wellspring of experience (grappling with a concept and applying it to new circumstances). Reflecting on Richard Feynman's poem "Ode to a Flower," John Dewey (1934) draws a parallel that explains the common ground between true science and true art:

> Flowers can be enjoyed without knowing about the inter-actions of soil, air, moisture, and seeds of which they are the result. But they cannot be *understood* without taking just these interactions into account—and theory is a matter of understanding.

He goes on to say:

> It is a commonplace that we cannot direct, save accidentally, the growth and flowering of plants, however lovely and enjoyed, without understanding their causal conditions. It should be just a commonplace that esthetic understanding—as distinct from sheer personal

enjoyment—must start with the soil, air, and light out of which things esthetically admirable arise. And these conditions are the conditions and factors that make an ordinary experience complete.

How many times have we asked students to draw the parts of a flower without actually observing how the flower breathes, lives, gives life, and dies? How many times have we asked students to solve math problems about building a bridge, baking, shopping, or trains leaving the station without ever asking them to build, bake, shop, or create? We often get stuck in the rut of giving students activities to do instead of offering them experiences to transform learning.

Think back for a moment to when you yourself were a first grader. Do you remember the wonder and excitement of finding your desk? Your new backpack? Playing with your friends at recess and going on fun field trips? Do you also remember tuning the teacher out completely, your eyes crawling up the wall to the clock, wondering how time had managed to come to a complete stop?

The obsession with knowledge, facts, and standardization is seen in our system as measuring school success. Our standards for graduation and achievement communicate that we are more impressed by high test scores, good grades, a high GPA, compliant behavior, and perfect attendance. We track these measures of student success because they're easier to measure, more objective, and more quantifiable than less tangible achievements. At the same time, we are also telling students that we are impressed when they think outside the box, communicate effectively, display sincerity, lead with integrity, and persevere. But we only reward the former set of achievements, not the latter. These mixed messages can create resentment in our students (and anxiety for us as we try to deal with and explain all the whys and why nots). Worse, not only does the first list measure just a select few intelligences, it measures them poorly.

The first list measures a student's ability to be compliant and follow the rules. A student could check everything off the first list and nothing in the second list, but in our current measures for success, we'd label that student high achieving, an honor student, ready for the "real world." As educators, we know that this isn't necessarily true. Albert Einstein, Winston Churchill, Bill Gates, Steve Jobs, Elton John, J. K. Rowling, and Whoopi Goldberg are just a few examples of very successful people who have stated in interviews that they did not get high marks in compliance during their school days, faced failure, rejection, and hardship, and who would not have checked off many items from the top list.

We often alienate the second list by labeling these as "twenty-first-century skills," or skills for success in life, but we clearly deprioritize them when we continue to base our whole accountability system on the first list and reward students accordingly. As leaders, we have a responsibility to redefine what it means to achieve, in a way that honors the natural learning process and the many differences that make us remarkable learners and human beings. If the second list of standards were more revered, more students would see themselves as achievers and would push themselves beyond the expectations set for them. And if we truly value the second list and find those skills to be more impressive indicators for success, we'll no longer say both lists are important. Instead, our actions will show we value creativity over credit, process over perfection, and growth over grades.

Today, we are teaching through an exciting time, as pedagogies change and we dismantle the status quo of traditional education. The rewriting of curriculum standards and the attention now placed on "twenty-first-century skills" are signs that we are moving beyond rote memorization. Just as companies are restructuring the way they work by incorporating virtual collaboration, increased teamwork, flexible hours, and flattened hierarchies, we should be reorganizing the structure of learning. Not only does this prepare students for the world outside of school, it also influences the world outside of the classroom.

When we redesign classroom learning structures, we can do so with an aim of increasing creative learning. This occurs when we can link existing concepts to one another in brand-new ways, create a new sequence of thinking, spawn new ideas and new ways of interacting, and incorporate new belief systems based on new evidence. Redesigning this structure means that the teacher is no longer at the front of the room expecting students to consume information or pay attention. It means that classroom time includes more hands-on creativity, student-to-student discourse, communication with experts using technology, and continual question asking.

An important lesson-design element found in many educational frameworks is the activation of prior knowledge. As teachers, how do we restructure the way we are activating prior knowledge without telling students how they should be experiencing it? We must let students experience it themselves, live the context, and thus absorb the experiences into their own new knowledge, forging new neural patterns. This means getting students outside or using technology to explore a new place.

Scarecrow thought he didn't have a brain because he didn't think in the same linear way as his companions. In a similar vein, much of what we discover was only really hidden around the corner, trying to fit into our existing worldview (e.g., I must be this kind of teacher because I'm different than the other teachers down the hall). Things that don't make sense occur to us as fragments or puzzle pieces that don't quite fit. They were only ever unnoticed analogies, possibly illogical, and made more sense when discovered as a result of imagination and emotion.

The Fighting Trees

Around the clock, 365 days per year, even during their time off, teachers face the overwhelming pressures and demands of an education system that seems intent on pulling the rug out from under them every time they almost find their footing. And, as if being the central part of a constantly changing landscape of expectation was not already enough, teachers are also expected to be innovative and creative amidst the constant avalanche of unrelenting initiatives, mandates, and the well-intentioned and almost always ill-timed "good idea," a perennial favorite. Given this barrage of daily challenges, how can teachers channel their creativity, grow their leadership skills, and develop high-level thinking?

In the classic 1939 film adaptation, the fighting trees are enchanted anthropomorphic apple trees who take a decidedly negative view of anyone who tries picking their apples. Hungry from her trip down the yellow brick road, Dorothy, new to the Land of Oz and not yet aware of the full range of its magical citizens, stops to pick a few apples but soon finds, to her chagrin, that the trees will not give up their treasures without a fight.

Scarecrow and Dorothy manage to escape easily because Scarecrow devises a simple plan and, by turning the trees' bad tempers to his advantage, once again saves the day. The Scarecrow's capacity to think on his toes, in the midst of uncertainty, and create a solution is a skill that keeps our new friends moving forward on their path. Philosopher and educator John Dewey wrote about this capacity in his 1910 treatise *How We Think*:

> Thinking begins in what may fairly enough be called a *forked-road situation*, a situation which is ambiguous, which presents a dilemma, which proposes alternatives. As long as our activity glides smoothly along from one thing to another, or as long as we permit our imagination to entertain fancies at pleasure, there is no call for reflection. Difficulty or obstruction in the way of reaching a belief brings us, however, to a pause. In the suspense of uncertainty, we metaphorically climb a tree; we try to find some standpoint from which we may survey

additional facts and, getting a more commanding view of the situation, may decide how the facts stand related to one another.

The whole reason we ever reflect is because something either echoes and calls to us from the depths of a prior experience, or we find a current experience perplexing or intriguing and seek to unravel its significance. Information that confirms what we already believe passes through our brain without any awareness, but when something contradicts our predetermined view of the world, scrutiny kicks into action. Exercise your brain with reflection, questioning, and openness, and model this for your students.

The Emerald City lies at the end of the beautiful yellow brick road for Dorothy and team, but just staying on the path isn't enough to help them achieve their goals. They soon discover that they must face not only unknown obstacles but also their own fears as they navigate the best way to move forward. By choosing to embrace uncertainty, we open ourselves up

> By choosing to embrace uncertainty, we open ourselves up to the possibility of more ways of thinking (I don't have to accept this reality because there is another way of doing it that will lead to more meaningful and fulfilling experiences), driving us to reflect and seek knowledge. The way we resolve discomfort or frustration is through reflection and deliberation.

to the possibility of more ways of thinking (I don't have to accept this reality because there is another way of doing it that will lead to more meaningful and fulfilling experiences), driving us to reflect and seek knowledge. The way we resolve discomfort or frustration is through reflection and deliberation. This kind of boundless thinking hinges on visualizing the interaction of new ideas with old ideas (e.g., eliminating daily lesson plans and co-creating unit project plans instead, or eliminating grade levels in school and creating a competency-based system instead) and requires a certain comfort with uncertainty. We need a system of curiosity built on this interaction of new ideas with the old way of doing school and a willingness for depth at a gradual pace.

Expand Your Thinking

1) What is one new thing you will intentionally try this month? Does it build on something you're currently doing?
2) What current way of teaching or thinking do you want to keep and what do you want to abandon?
3) How will you create white space (taking walks in nature, doing hobbies you enjoy, having quiet time, etc.) in your day?
4) List three challenges you're currently facing in the classroom. How can you learn from them? Can you use them to your advantage?

So many problems and obstacles are difficult because they challenge a teacher's paradigm or current ways of thinking. That's why it's important to open your mind to improvising and changing so you can successfully solve problems and face challenges with courage. Developing innovative solutions, adjusting your decisions based on new evidence, reconsidering your beliefs and values, and shifting your perspective are all valuable ways to address challenges.

Authentic Learning: Nathan's Experience

I recall a childhood memory very vividly. Growing up in the South, I remember the oh-so-familiar sounds of the singing cicadas in the summer. One day, I had the opportunity to watch the fascinating phenomenon of a cicada transforming into an adult by shedding its skin. It was truly exciting to observe the transformation as it unfolded over the course of about an hour. I had always seen their exoskeletons clinging to the trunks of trees, but never the actual process of metamorphosis. The experience was so intriguing to me, in part because it was brand new, but at the same time ordinary. I had never stopped to notice this natural phenomenon even though it happened all the time, all around me. The intersection of the a-ha moment with my natural curiosity and awe became a noteworthy learning experience. And it happened through the process of learning by experience.

Just watch a spider spin a web or a butterfly choose its flower. Creatures explore, solve problems, develop solutions, and take risks. What they do isn't simply for fun and entertainment; they undertake these activities to build the skills they need to survive. Their daily experiences are fundamental to evolution, and without that, most of our world wouldn't exist. By watching the cicada shed its skin, I realized how many opportunities to learn were all around me. It wasn't until I had the space to play and discover that I was allowed to be me and fully encapsulated in what I was seeing around me.

As we have seen, the Scarecrow's experiences along the yellow brick road, while taking him out of his comfort zone, built and fortified his knowledge and skills, propelling the development of his problem-solving ability and creativity. Teachers, both novice and veteran, find comfort in the realization that anything of real and worthwhile value will take time and experience. There is no such thing as overnight success. However, just because a teacher is brand new doesn't mean they will have to teach for years and years before they are able to experience success. Conversely, a seasoned teacher with decades of career experience can also fall into ruts and rituals, relying on "what has always worked," which may or may not be conducive to forward momentum. Everyone brings their life experiences to the classroom, and reflection, combined with openness and the ability to embrace growth, can help teachers build on those prior experiences to make better decisions. Every day is a new opportunity to gain experience, to create something exciting, and to realize the potential of our experiences to create lasting change in our classrooms and the world. And it's exactly in these challenges of designing, creating, risk taking, and revising where the magic unfolds in the making of a teacher's character and destiny.

Wisdom can sometimes fall out of a clear blue sky, when least expected, and sometimes far too late (if you are, say, a wicked witch who dwells in the East and has a thing for magic shoes), but for most of us, wisdom is the result of hard work, intention, opportunities, and experiences.

And sometimes, as is the case for our friend Scarecrow, wisdom is simply waiting for us to notice and embrace it, just outside the comfortable boundaries of a forgotten cornfield in a corner of the magical Land of Oz.

"I shall take the heart," returned the Tin Woodman; "for brains do not make one happy, and happiness is the best thing in the world."

—L. Frank Baum,
The Wonderful Wizard of Oz

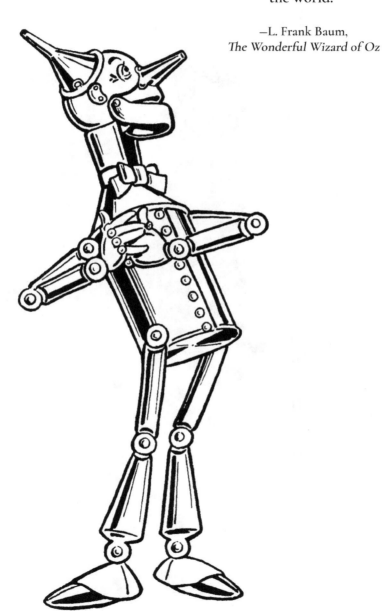

3

Heart: Tin Man

In Oz, after meeting the Scarecrow, Dorothy next befriends the Tin Woodman, whom she finds rusted in the forest. Caught in the rain and unable to move, the Tin Man has spent "more than a year" immobile and unable to help himself. Like the Tin Woodman, many of us find that after semesters and years of doing what we thought was expected of us, or what was dictated to us by the school system, we become numb to why we started teaching in the first place. We become stiff and rigid, frozen in place—unable to help ourselves. Some days we struggle to find the heart of teaching.

Much of what is required of teachers can take the fun and love out of teaching. As Nathan travels across the country, observing teachers in their classrooms and listening to their experiences, he's often heard this said: "Teachers don't know what they don't know." What a demeaning and limiting approach. As a young teacher, there were many times Nathan and his colleagues were made to feel that they were inadequate because the professional development seminars they were required to attend told them what they were doing was wrong and that they should have been doing some things differently. We believe, however, that an effective professional development session is not designed to show us what we don't know. Rather, professional development should harness our creativity, nurture our interest in personal growth, illuminate our strengths, and help us build on what we already know.

We've already mentioned our garden at home in Maine. We were thrilled in the initial phases of mapping out the gardens and planting our fruit trees, roses, and vegetables. After years of living in big cities, we were finally free to have the blossoming garden of our dreams. However, when late spring and early summer approached, the infamous Maine black flies and mosquitos decided to join the party. We had to bathe in repellant just to go outside to get the newspaper, lest we succumb to the vampiric invasion that had descended on us. This extra annoyance ate away at our excitement over gardening. Additionally, with the warmer weather also came an explosion of poison ivy. Surrounding the house as if to keep us prisoners, it encroached on all the nature paths we had cleared in the spring and threatened to strangle our perennial garden in its obnoxious death grip. It was yet another obstacle keeping us from fully enjoying our garden. The last major barrier we faced was higher-than-average rainfall. Our newly planted blueberry bushes were drowning, and there wasn't much we could do to save them. Our excitement for gardening had waned significantly. But thankfully, hope still remained on the horizon, just waiting patiently for us in the form of one beautiful, mild, low-humidity day in the garden—reminding us of the joys of gardening and providing a renewed sense of purpose and determination to overcome our gardening roadblocks. We had to ask ourselves: What is it about the gardening journey that we love? What energizes us about maintaining it? Do we really have the heart for gardening, or is it just something that sounds fun but isn't really *us* at the end of the day?

This same scenario often unfolds in our teaching journey, and we have to ask ourselves the same questions:

- Do we truly have the heart for teaching? For students? For learning?
- What about your teaching and learning journey have you truly loved thus far? What experiences have energized you or made your soul happy?

Once we have identified that we have perhaps rusted in place like the Tin Man, that we have become disconnected and desensitized, we are then free to rediscover what first drew us to education. We must rediscover our love—our heart—for teaching.

Perhaps the most moving part of the Tin Woodman's story and, by extension, our story as educators, is that we were never really without our hearts to begin with. We can remember and reconnect with our hearts by better understanding and liberating ourselves, discovering what it was about influential educators and leaders in our lives that inspired us, emulating those qualities, and creating professional learning opportunities for ourselves, our students, our colleagues, and our communities that not only equip and support but also renew our sense of heart for teaching.

Liberation

If we are lucky, there comes a point when we no longer wish to blend in with the masses. We let ourselves off the hook by reflecting on why we were a part of something that wasn't intrinsically *us* to begin with. Maybe it was easier to just go with the flow. Maybe all of the other teachers in our grade level or subject level followed a certain classroom behavior plan or a specific instructional framework. Maybe we thought our principal expected something from us and we didn't want to disappoint them. But something, some event or realization, opened our eyes (maybe it's this book) to this reality: You're not being yourself. *It is now time to be yourself.* Fully. Completely. Authentically. Our students want and need to see the real us. How else can we expect them to be their true selves if we're not willing to do so and cannot give them an example and working map?

Philosopher Friedrich Nietzsche (1965) said, "No one can build you the bridge on which you, and only you, must cross the river of life. There may be countless trails and bridges and demigods who would gladly carry you across; but only at the price of pawning and forgoing yourself. There is one path in the world that none can walk but you. Where does it lead? Don't ask, walk!"

Remembering Your Why: Nathan's Experience

I remember my first job as a science teacher and how pivotal those first years were in walking my own path. Every beginning teacher has an idea of the kind of teacher they will be. After studying pedagogy in college and gaining some student teaching experience, I envisioned a collaborative classroom with a lot of exploration, discovery, and experiments, as I believed that was how science (or any subject, for that matter) is best learned. Then I was confronted with four different subjects (also referred to as "preps") I had to teach, along with a myriad of extracurricular responsibilities, faculty meetings, etc. Because it was easier (and frankly, it's how the masses kept up), I started allowing the textbook to determine the scope and sequence of my lesson plans. Additionally, the classroom was built as a lecture-style room with tiered seating, making small groups almost impossible. I felt myself falling into a rut, with my energy and passion starting to slowly drain away. I vividly remember the moment it all changed. A student walked into class and proclaimed, "This class is boring." That hurt. In knee-jerk fashion, I said, "Okay, what do you want to do today?" The student answered, "I want to go outside." I said, "All right, let's go outside."

Thinking quickly on my feet about how the lesson planned for the day would work outside, I realized I now had to throw out my plans. I had recently become certified to test water quality and already had outdoor kits organized. That day I took my students down to the nearby bayou, and we tested it for E. coli, phosphates, algae, etc. The students had a blast and could finally see connections to what they were doing in the lab. That day changed the course of teaching for me. Not only was I determined that students would never be bored again, but every day would be an opportunity to actively learn in meaningful and fun ways. I grew up that day. I wasn't going to succumb to what was easiest or what the masses were doing. I remembered why I had become an educator: to make a difference.

Expand Your Thinking

1) What keeps people from being their true selves?
2) Do I have a fear of not being liked?
3) Do I have a fear of someone else seeing my insecurity?
4) Do I have a fear of being embarrassed? Maybe even a fear of being fired (a pervasive, irrational, self-created fear)?

The feeling of being trapped in a situation leads to a feeling of hope-lessness and sucks the joy out of teaching (and life). And just like the Tin Man, you may have the misfortune of being stuck for years in the same position, unable to move or change.

Many teachers may place an unnecessary burden on themselves to appear to have expertise in all aspects of teaching, beyond their own abilities or interests. Even though we may hear that our job as teach-ers is to work alongside students to illuminate strengths and identify growth opportunities, we can't help but give credence to fears and question ourselves. *What if my students (or colleagues) learn that I've never taught this grade or subject before? What if my students (or colleagues) learn that I had to take the teacher certification test multiple times? Will my colleagues label me as old-school, set in my ways and obsolete, because of my many years of experience? Will my colleagues not affirm my skills as an effective teacher because I'm a brand-new teacher without as much experience as they think I should have?*

Teachers have not traditionally been given a voice to express concerns or share problems with school leaders. In toxic school cultures, leaders have even labeled teachers who share their concerns as *troublemakers* or *pot stirrers*. School leaders must make transparency and equity guiding principles and a building norm to create a healthy problem-solving culture and a healthy culture for teachers to truly be themselves. Equity means school leaders are committed to developing environments, systems, and practices in ways that provide educators with what they need based on careful attention to the particulars of an educator's situation. Modeling this kind of no-holds-barred mentality in which everything is fair game for discussion can turn a stagnant culture into a liberating one that hinges on open communication, sincere relationships, and trusted leaders.

Influential People

Most of us chose education as a career because we had an influential teacher or mentor who believed in us. Their affirmation, guidance, and support had a profound, journey-altering impact on our life and our life choices. We wanted to have that kind of impact on the lives of others, so we chose teaching. Alternatively, we might have had an unpleasant experience, like the one Herbie mentioned earlier with that particularly tricky box, and we used an experienced injustice as the driver to make a difference in our world. Reflecting on educators and mentors that have helped to liberate us can have a profound impact on how we view ourselves as change agents in education and grant us the heretofore slumbering gift of reciprocating the outpouring of light and warmth, happiness and joy we've experienced along the way.

The Role of Great Mentors: Nathan's Experience

Given the impact my high school chemistry teacher had on me, it's no surprise that I later became a chemistry teacher myself! But the lab experiments and hair-sizzling demonstrations aren't what I remember most, although these were much more exciting school experiences compared to the annoying homework and endless note taking. It was the energy, fun, laughter, and excitement that the teacher purposely cultivated in class. Ionic compounds took on human characteristics, and drawings on the board were purposefully humorous. My teacher found ways to incorporate students' names into chemistry problems and made everyone feel like a star rather than simply a number in a vast sea of ever-rotating high school students. Learning was made enjoyable, and even though chemistry was fifth period—right before lunch, when we were starving as only high schoolers can be—the class was always surprised at how fast the time flew by.

When I entered college, I initially didn't plan on getting a degree in chemistry education. I wanted to be a weatherman, but the university I ended up choosing did not have an undergraduate meteorology program. So instead, I chose chemistry education with teacher licensure, with the intention of getting my master's in meteorology after I graduated. But once I enrolled in the program, I found how gratifying it was to help other chemistry students. As I approached my senior year, I became a chemistry lab teaching assistant, as I found that I loved to be in the lab with my fellow students while they were conducting experiments. The best part was watching students discover an unknown substance or create an unexpected chemical reaction with the awareness that I had created those conditions for students to discover science in new and exciting ways. Years later, I sat down and wrote a thank-you letter to my high-school chemistry teacher expressing the deep gratitude I felt for an experience that forever altered the course of my life.

---❁---

Who in your education journey helped cultivate your creativity? Who went out of their way to make you feel valued and affirmed your individuality? Who inspired you to become a teacher, and how does their influence live on today?

---❁---

Who in your education journey helped cultivate your creativity? Who went out of their way to make you feel valued and affirmed your individuality? Who inspired you to become a teacher, and how does their influence live on today? These questions can help remind us of the influential people in our lives and why we chose education as a career path and lifelong mission. These questions can help you find your heart again, just as the Tin Man rediscovered his.

Professional Learning That Renews

Teaching is a profession that combines the creative spirit of an artist with the logistical acumen of an engineer. Additionally, teachers are responsible for groups of students, so in a sense they're also like pseudo-entrepreneurs. In this context, teachers are guiding, supporting, and facilitating opportunities for students to lead, think creatively, and collaborate together.

Most of us would agree that teachers require a high level of independence and autonomy so that they can be their most creative selves. This level of creativity stokes the fire of our passion for teaching and learning. Unfortunately, professional development (PD) often works against this philosophy. Many times it's forced upon teachers as a matter of compliance, which doesn't give them the freedom to choose how they will engage with new learning opportunities.

When I ask teachers who feel content and rewarded in their work, who feel they get to exercise a high level of creative capacity in their schools, what factor best contributes to this environment, they indicate that it is in fact a high degree of autonomy. They report being encouraged to choose the professional learning that best enabled them to develop curiosity about concepts applicable to them at their own pace, without overbearing supervision or PD mandates from their principal. These empowering leaders instead happily granted educators the freedom to explore their own professional learning journey and encouraged them to make classroom decisions on their own or with their teams.

Teaching with one's whole heart requires a combination of creativity, continuous learning opportunities, skill, knowledge, commitment, and enthusiasm—traits that when fully operational and synchronized launch these remarkable educators on heartfelt missions to excel and enjoy the fruits of their commitment to a meaningful experience, providing them with a way to demonstrate their skills and self-worth to themselves first and foremost. We often hear "students first" or "do what's right for kids." These cliché and overused statements, although needed at a time when many in education have lost sight of this vision, can make teachers feel like they have to sacrifice themselves in order to be good teachers. This is simply not true. Of course caring for students is our mission, and of course the well-being of our students is why we are in the classroom, but we won't be able to care for our students if we are not caring for ourselves.

Professional learning must also give teachers the opportunity to be courageous in their teaching practices. (More on courage in the next chapter when we meet the Lion!) What do we mean here? For example, Dave Burgess created "hooks" in his book *Teach Like a Pirate* so teachers can make their lessons outrageously entertaining, engaging, and powerful. He provides a variety of different hooks, some centered around music and art, and some around storytelling and technology. If a teacher, by nature, is more reserved, initially they might reject having students create raps to articulate thinking. But if a professional learning experience invites them to step outside their comfort zone, they may be willing to try something new and engaging that they might have otherwise not tried. Professional learning can renew your passion for teaching if you're willing to explore new ways of creating learning experiences in your classroom.

Expand Your Thinking

1) Has your zeal or passion for teaching diminished at points in your career? Has it gone away completely? Journal about these experiences.
2) Have there been times in your teaching career when you were unable to articulate your purpose for teaching? If so, write about them.
3) Consider, as you review your responses to the above questions, what circumstances or attitudes you've needed to change to free yourself, which influences have given you the courage and inspiration to change, and how professional learning can support you as you rediscover your heart for teaching and learning.

Self-Care: Nathan's Experience

When I was a school administrator, I learned about self-care the hard way. During the week, so much was going on in the school day that I never had time to "get it all done." On top of that, I was getting my doctorate, which meant the only time I had to write, catch up on emails, work on plans and projects, etc., were my nights and weekends. When

Monday rolled around, I often resented myself for choosing to work all weekend. At the time, it seemed like that was what a good leader did in the school system—worked all the time. How else was it all going to get done? Over time, my stress became overwhelming. I noticed that I wasn't being my best self. How could I? I didn't even know myself anymore because I had buried myself in work. One particular weekend I decided I had had enough and called a friend and mentor. He told me, "The work will never be done, but working like you are, YOU will be soon." I realized in that moment how right he was. I started to create boundaries between myself and the twenty-four-hour workday. I began to be purposeful about creating space for myself. I realized that the secret to being the best leader you can be is to take care of yourself and your own happiness.

The secret to being your best during the week is to practice self-care. Below are some simple but powerful things you can do to be your best self at work and at home:

- Acknowledge your strengths
- Protect your time
- Nurture your inner life
- Seek solitude
- Read for pleasure
- Take strolls
- Turn off your notifications (They aren't going anywhere. You won't miss a thing. They'll be there waiting for you, but you will be emotionally stronger and more equipped at efficiently dealing with them when you prioritize your own well-being first.)

My mentor also told me to "pull my own happiness wagon." Today, I still live by that quote. My happiness doesn't depend on other people or external forces, but solely on my attitude and choices.

Do you want to reignite your fire for teaching? Are you ready to break free and dust off all the corrosion of inactive compliance? Just as the Tin Man must keep his joints continuously well-oiled to move about freely, we can all renew our purpose and find our hearts again by rediscovering the joy in the classroom. To continue to thrive in the face of our daily challenges, we must all learn how to keep the "rust" at bay.

"All the other animals in the forest naturally expect me to be brave, for the Lion is everywhere thought to be the King of Beasts . . ."

"You have plenty of courage, I am sure," answered Oz. "All you need is confidence in yourself. There is no living thing that is not afraid when it faces danger. True courage is in facing danger when you are afraid, and that kind of courage you have in plenty."

—L. Frank Baum, *The Wonderful Wizard of Oz*

4

Courage: Lion

ions traditionally symbolize the epitome of courage. Throughout the history of art and literature, lions exemplify the height and breadth of bravery and nobility. It is through this lens of expectation that the Cowardly Lion believes that his fear somehow makes him inferior, that it somehow negates his value and makes him less than he ought to be. When he first meets Dorothy and her two new friends, and joins their journey down the yellow brick road, he does not yet realize that having courage doesn't mean the complete absence of fear—it means acting in spite of or perhaps even because of fear, which he already does frequently. Only after the Wizard grants the Lion a physical reminder and celebration of his courage does he finally begin to *feel* brave. He didn't yet know that you can be both very courageous while also being openly, and honestly, afraid.

Bringing Courage into the Classroom: Nathan's Experience

When I became a teacher, I didn't quite realize the level of courage I'd need. It takes courage, for example, to establish a classroom community of norms for students, or to confront a teacher down the hall who's creating a classroom environment that doesn't promote positive behavior. I also underestimated the value of courage when I became an administrator. It takes courage to address instructional practices that are antiquated and ineffective, and to have a productive conversation with a teacher who lacks the motivation to be a team player. When I started in these roles, my passion and excitement masked the fears I managed to tuck away. Within just a few days, I had to tap into my courage to deal with challenging situations. As a twenty-seven-year-old administrator, though I had diligently worked hard, tried my hardest to actively listen to teachers, and read all the leadership books I could get my hands on, I still didn't necessarily feel *prepared* to make the kinds of decisions I had to make. School leaders will tell you that not only do you have to make wise decisions in the midst of challenging situations, but many times you're making those decisions quickly. (Think safety drills, emergencies, a substitute teacher who didn't show up, etc.) As a school leader, my priorities were to build relationships and trust with teachers, students, and parents, to care for the well-being of all, and to have sincere conversations about how we could transform learning in our school. My passion for learning, knowledge of instructional strategies, and empathy for my students were essential qualities, but they were not enough to make me a successful leader.

As I navigated the challenges of being a school leader, I eventually began to discover who I was as a person and as a leader. Every time I exercised my voice as a leader, I became more confident and found more courage.

The Cowardly Lion unknowingly possessed all the courage he would ever need; he just needed someone to affirm it, to show him he already possessed it. The same is true for educators: we have all the courage we need. We have to continually act with bravery—doing the right thing and even the risky thing, even though we're scared, timid, or hesitant. Courage is actualized in the classroom and in our collaborative school environments through our willingness to take on conflict, welcome criticism, establish complete transparency and healthy relationships, and communicate our purpose.

> ❈
> Courage is actualized in the classroom and in our collaborative school environments through our willingness to take on conflict, welcome criticism, establish complete transparency and healthy relationships, and communicate our purpose.
> ❈

Conflict

Conflict is guaranteed when you're working with other people. What's not guaranteed is how conflict will be handled within each team or school community. When faced with tough opposition in the midst of change, we might become defensive and guarded, placing a barrier between ourselves and the person opposing us. Or we might tend to remain quiet, resorting to a passive-aggressive silent treatment as a response. During conflict, we may play out our own internal, self-created, and cyclical drama—we might stonewall in an attempt to avoid uncomfortable conversations knowing that engaging in emotional discussion will only result in a hostile confrontation. Or maybe we tend to respond to conflict by launching personal attacks when we feel slighted. None of these conflict management strategies promotes healthy dialogue in teams or, indeed, anywhere else in life. *Manage* is a better word than *resolve* in this instance because conflict in relationships is natural and has functional, positive aspects that can provide opportunities for people to grow in collaboration and in understanding. It takes courage to tackle conflict head on. Conflict management experts John and Julie Gottman, of the Gottman Institute, say that it is not the *appearance* of conflict but rather how it's *managed* that predicts the success or failure of a relationship. They provide antidotes to aid in conflict management:

1. Talk about your feelings using "I" statements and express a positive need, e.g., "I felt my voice wasn't heard when my ideas were not acknowledged during the team meeting."

2. Remind yourself of the other person's positive qualities and express positive gratitude, e.g., "I understand that you've been swamped with so many leadership responsibilities, but could you please remember to accept or decline my calendar invite? I'd appreciate it."

3. Accept the other person's perspective and offer an apology for any wrongdoing, e.g., "I understand your class can get rambunctious, and I could lighten up a little."

4. When tempted to withdraw from conflict, take a break and do something else for a bit, e.g., "I'm feeling overwhelmed and I need to take a break. Can you give me twenty minutes and then we can talk about this?"

It takes courage to be able to recognize conflict for what it is, and to manage the many disparate pieces of it before they spin out of control, but being vigilant in your self-awareness goes a long way in maintaining healthy relationships and boundaries.

Many times, conflict arises out of criticism. The capacity for criticism to hurt or help is proportional to its context and intent. If you display hostility in your demeanor, your communication will be seen as an attack. Even if what you have to say is the best and most helpful guidance, if it is perceived as aggressive, you will most likely go unheard. Conversely, if your intent is to help guide with sincerity and

Courage: Lion

empathy, then you may have some hope of being heard. Criticism can be constructive, but how do we get to a place where we're okay with it and, dare we say, even welcome it?

Welcoming Criticism Courageously

No one ever said that making decisions would be easy. It is not a practice for the faint of heart. On one side of the coin, decisions have the power to change and expand horizons in every possible direction, and on the other, they open up the decision-maker to a universe of opinions and judgment. With every single decision we make comes risk. When we make a decision, some of our colleagues may praise, while others may judge and critique—even more so if we're in leadership positions, or if the stakes are elevated by the influence and scale of our decisions, or if we find ourselves challenging the status quo. The reality of criticism being leveled at us daily is almost guaranteed. For new school leaders in particular, not having a knee-jerk reaction or an exaggerated response to a complaint or criticism can be challenging. We've all experienced that dreaded moment when a colleague reaches out with "I have a concern . . ." Our reaction, however, need not be one of doom and gloom. We don't have to fall apart, become unhinged, take it personally, or see it as a threat. We are not made of glass.

Processing Non-Constructive Criticism: Herbie's Experience

In our house, as in every other home around the world, Nathan and I each take on different roles depending on daily situations, people, and issues that need to be addressed. However, we do have a cardinal, unspoken, inviolable rule: we are always on each other's side. No matter what, we always know that we will support each other unconditionally and without judgment. But beyond our home, our family, and its needs, we have our own unique and very different personalities, each with their own specific experiences and strengths. Nathan has a very optimistic, forgiving, and sunny nature—one which always sees the good in situations, and opportunities for forward-moving development—while I, well . . . let's just say I tend to go the other way. Quite vocally. And quite often.

That notwithstanding, I have recently, and quite accidentally, introduced a new phrase in the house that has become a kind of game of sorts. To wit: we recently experienced our very first autumn in our new home in New England. Having been born on the coast of Southern California, on the exact opposite side of the country, I had never before witnessed the exploding cascades of reds and golds unfolding outside our windows, the landscape changing wildly each day. And so, naturally, I posted on Instagram what I thought was a lovely shot of the changing leaves on the ash and maple trees outside my office. I immediately received a text message from an ex-colleague that could only have been interpreted as negative. They remarked at how boring and simple I was that I found joy in something as "basic" as a tree. Their comments, though wearing the guise of a joke, actually only thinly veiled their own jealous and petty personality. However, by a happy accidental twist of fate, this person's intention was washed away at once when I made the random off-hand remark (as I am far too often wont to make): "I have no reaction."

Boom! Where did that come from? I am quite sure that those words have never before passed my lips. I am definitely more prone to hyperbolic, dramatic overreaction than Nathan. But there it was: "I have no reaction." Try it. I promise you will be shocked at the astounding power of the simple phrase. True to my word, I had no reaction, and we now invoke our new Phrase-Of-Power regularly. When you are aware of the power of other people's opinions, reactions, and judgments, you can negate any impact by choosing not to interact. My mother always said, "Do not water the weeds, my love, unless you want them to grow."

Reclaiming Your Courage in the Face of Criticism

We aren't suggesting that criticism be dismissed and disregarded altogether. As a matter of fact, criticism can sometimes be more helpful than affirmation as we seek to gain valuable and honest perspectives from trusted and credible sources. However, you can confidently disregard criticism that's aimed at tearing you down (from people who are sometimes referred to as "haters") rather than giving genuine feedback for growth. As we mentioned earlier, criticism can be helpful or hurtful depending on the specific intent of the person giving it, and how we choose to receive it.

One thing is certain: how to relate to criticism in a healthy way is an essential survival skill both in leadership and in life. We can find a healthy equilibrium when we are able to identify criticism as an opportunity to see someone else's perspective, to listen, and to grow; or, conversely, when we are able to accurately identify when it is appropriate to smile and nod, offer a polite "Thank you," and continue on with our day unaffected. Sometimes criticism might simply be a reflection of someone's insecurities; it can also be an expression of jealousy. This is something for the other person to resolve, and not for you to take personally. In other words, it is simply not your business to figure it out, or to interact with it. Leave it alone and continue on your merry way. You are too busy being your own fabulous, unique "you." You have too much else going on, too many other things of real value that need your attention and precious energy. Don't water those weeds! This approach is not for the faint of heart, but for the courageous.

What happens when you get criticism from a "hater"? With no basis or justification for their claim, they will lob their best negativity and their own issues squarely into your space. The best way to deal with haters is to transform them from your foes into your fans. This takes courage and wit to pull off, but everyone wins in the end. Before you turn a hater into a fan, ask yourself first if this is worth your time. If it's a random Internet troll who spends all their time attacking others just for the sake of the battle, don't waste a single second. If it's someone you have to interact with on a regular basis, consider a different approach.

How do you do this? How can you transform a foe into a fan? You affirm *them*. When Nathan was a school leader, there was a teacher who was skeptical about his leadership abilities because of his age and youthful appearance—things that were beyond his control, and utterly irrelevant. So he approached the teacher and asked if they would like to be on a leadership team, as their experiences and thinking would offer new perspectives to the group. The teacher, shocked and surprised, accepted his offer. From that point on, he received nothing but respect and positive vibes from this teacher.

We want to make it clear that you are not welcoming criticism from bullies, trolls, and online haters. You have the right to tell your truth while living freely, fully, wildly, and full of energy, laughter, and love. Completely disregard the haters and give no energy or power to them. We acknowledge, of course, that this is easier said than done. Mathematician and psychologist Vi Hart explains, "I have no power over you that you don't give me, and you have no power over me that I don't give you. Your greatest creation is yourself. Like any great work of art, creating a great self means putting in hard work, every day, for years." Additionally, we love the way Maria Popova, of the arts and culture website Brainpickings.org, reframes the famous quote from Maya Angelou, "When someone shows you who they are, believe them the first time." As Popova says, "Just as importantly, however, when people try to tell you who *you* are, *don't* believe them. You are the only custodian of your own integrity, and the assumptions made by those who misunderstand who you are and what you stand for reveal a great deal about them and absolutely nothing about you."

One other vital component of successfully dealing with criticism, and with someone who is only interested in playing the villain role in your life, is your sense of humor. Never underestimate the importance of not taking anything too seriously. Let them do their worst, while you remain your best. If someone is just absolutely dead set on being a little black rain cloud, day after endless day, wish them well, hope for their well-being, and move on. Nothing and no one is ever worth your happiness and peace of mind. Full stop.

Establishing Trust and Transparency through Healthy Relationships

One of our favorite go-to clips we most enjoy rewatching and sharing is the famous *I Love Lucy* chocolate factory scene. If you've never seen it, stop everything and go search for the video. At first, the little chocolates, slowly easing their way down the conveyor belt, seem easy enough to manage, and Lucy and Ethel are able to keep up the appearance that they have everything under control. But when the conveyor belt speeds up and they struggle to wrap all the now faster-moving chocolates, they begin hiding pieces of candy in their hats and shoving them in their mouths. The supervisor comes in and, not seeing the hidden pieces of ruined chocolate, judges that the ladies might be more efficient at their job than she first surmised and declares: "Fine. You're doing splendidly." And then, of course, she piles on more work by calling out to the conveyor belt operator: "Speed it up!" Now, with the little chocolates racing down the conveyor belt at near light speed, the ladies are really in for a challenging time.

How many times have you had to "keep up appearances" by pretending you were "doing great," while you were actually feeling overwhelmed and stressed? Many of us fear that by being vulnerable, we will appear weak and unable to handle the pressures of work, teaching, and, later, the increased responsibilities and challenges of being a leader. There is also a fear of being treated differently or not being given challenging enough tasks because of a perceived lack of bandwidth to handle them.

Transparency and Trust: Nathan's Experience

In my second year as a teacher, I took a risk and began sharing my struggles of being vulnerable with a co-teacher. I found that she had some great solutions and thoughts that she offered without judgement. At the same time, she shared that she also had her own struggles and challenges, and I was reciprocally able to share my thoughts and ideas with her. We both decided to create a zone of trust where we felt safe to be vulnerable, and in the process both grew as teachers. We established a weekly check-in at the end of the day on Friday to ensure we were purposeful in establishing well-being and camaraderie. The same was true for my time as a school leader. I was able to be transparent about my fears and the problems I observed, and in return I received warmth, trust, and vulnerability from teachers. One way to do this is to send weekly pulse checks out to your staff and colleagues with the intent on gauging culture and what's working or not working. Additionally, making this feedback visible via an online collaborative document increases the level of transparency in the school community. Practicing transparency takes courage, but it also fosters your ability to tap into your courage. And when you are able to share the truth of your experiences and fears, everyone has the opportunity to grow and move forward together.

Purpose

Given a choice, of course many of us would rather focus on, dream about, and spend time doing something we feel passionate about, but passion alone does not give one the ability to lead with courage or take action. Though we are naturally attracted to the positive energy passionate people exude, because it affirms an inner joy and creates a pleasant emotion, passion can often be circumstantial and based on what excites someone at a particular point in his or her life, which may or may not be indicative of a broader experience. Parts of our personal lives and professional work may at times be banal and difficult, requiring self-discipline from us to deal with them appropriately. These challenges require us to have a strong sense of purpose, so we can endure them to achieve something larger.

In his book *Ego Is the Enemy*, Ryan Holiday (2017) shares that passion is *about* something. For example, "I am so passionate about education." Purpose is *to* and *for* something. For example, "I must lead with courage in order to positively impact education," or "I am wired to empathize with people in order to gain a better understanding of others," or "I must struggle through conflict management for the sake of healthy relationships and collaboration." Purpose is about giving time, resources, and energy to benefit something or someone besides oneself.

When one faces difficult challenges, passion can wane, whereas purpose becomes stronger. Passion gives you the motivation to wake up in the morning or plan that amazing lesson, but purpose represents *why* you teach and what will drive you onward even on the snowiest mornings when you would rather stay curled up by the fire, or through boring meetings when you know you could be working on something else. Knowing your purpose helps you speak with ease and sincerity, and with no hidden agenda, allowing you to communicate your thoughts and ideas honestly. A grounded purpose motivates you to seek feedback from trusted peers, to examine areas of individual growth, and to become more malleable each day as you encounter new facts and evidence. Teachers and leaders with a strong moral purpose feel comfortable in their own skin, have confidence in themselves, and honor their past experiences and journeys. They are humble and don't believe they are the smartest or the most experienced people in the room. They look outside themselves for new ways to improve teaching and learning. To gain new perspectives and knowledge, purpose-driven educators surround themselves with people who are different from them and who think differently than they do.

The Cowardly Lion learned that courage must ultimately come from within rather than from some external source. Like the Lion, we can sometimes be so ashamed of our fears, anxieties, and insecurities that we don't recognize our own innate courage.

It takes courage to step beyond the status quo and to keep going even when you're not sure where exactly that path will lead. Also know that there are times when it's difficult to find the courage you need to face conflict and criticism, and to live out your purpose. Seek out loved ones and supporters who will affirm you. It is always the right time to create a support team of people who believe in you, support you through good *and* challenging times, and who will keep you moving forward through their unconditional encouragement. Find comfort and inspiration in this sentence: You are brave enough, you are strong enough, and you, alone, just as you are, are enough.

The Wicked Witch laughed to herself, and thought, "I can still make her my slave, for she does not know how to use her power."

—L. Frank Baum, *The Wonderful Wizard of Oz*

5

Spirit: Dorothy

Dorothy Gale, as befitting the protagonist of a novel, possesses all the quintessential traits one might expect of a heroine: a spirit of gentleness, kindness, goodness, confidence, courage, determination, and an intrinsic calmness amid a landscape of constant change and conflict. Literally whisked away from her home in Kansas by way of a cyclone to a magical world, she quickly discovers dangers she could never have imagined as she embarks on a journey to the Emerald City with the singular goal of getting back home. On her way, she gets a new pair of enchanted shoes, learns how to battle the imminent threat of a wicked enemy, and exposes political dishonesty. Yet through it all, and even though she has a myriad of struggles of her own to navigate, she displays endless compassion and selflessness when it comes to the well-being of her new friends.

We all love and are inspired by Dorothy because we can all relate to her. She is us. We have all been that fish-out-of-water, thrown into an unknown situation, wanting only the comforts of home and familiar faces. Her determination to accomplish a goal in the midst of fear and

> Dorothy reminds us of our agency, our self-confidence, our intrinsic gifts as caretakers, and that we all have unique powers and talents that no one else has, and which some may covet.

the unknown, and her desire to help a friend discover a gift they already possess, resonate with our own ambitions. Dorothy reminds us of our agency, our self-confidence, our intrinsic gifts as caretakers, and that we all have unique powers and talents that no one else has, and which some may covet. The Wicked Witch of the West self-destructs over her jealousy and avarice. Her madness to gain control of Dorothy's shoes blinds her to reason and fatally leads to her own end.

We Are in Control of Our Destiny

After getting blown away, quite literally, to Oz by a cyclone, Dorothy, in one single clarifying moment, immediately knows exactly what she wants. This is a crucial point to note: Dorothy is motivated by one singular goal—to get back home to Kansas, to her Aunt Em. This is her primary drive. How many times have we found ourselves in a new place and known, with absolute certainty, that it is not where we want to be but lack the courage, support, and/or direction needed to get where we want to go? How can we find our way home? As soon as Dorothy experiences the stark reality and complete isolation of what living in Oz represents, she knows immediately what she wants to do. In that one moment of self-truth, all her thoughts are galvanized into one single focus. But how does she get home? She knows what she wants, but how does she fulfill this goal? When she asks for help, she is sent to ask the mysterious Wizard for guidance, and this isn't a journey that she necessarily wants to make. Additionally, when she reaches the Emerald City, the Wizard says that he will only help her (and her friends) conditionally if she kills the Wicked Witch of the West, and Dorothy doesn't want to go anywhere near the Witch, let alone kill her.

Throughout her tenure in Oz, Dorothy is dispatched by different characters to different places to accomplish numerous objectives— none of which she really *wants* to accomplish. She must continually react and adapt to the circumstances, a situation educators can no doubt relate to. We, too, must react to initiatives and mandates as they are passed down because, in the moment, we may feel like we have no choice. When educators are expected to comply with changes they don't agree with, the change itself will suffer (as will the well-being of the teacher). And when teachers feel blocked from having input in district and schoolwide decision-making, morale and confidence erode. The path "home," to that place where we feel understood and seen, becomes harder to find.

A leadership study conducted in 2007 by Greg Cameron and Tim Waters of Mid-continent Research for Education and Learning (McREL) concluded that four school leadership responsibilities, culture, communication, input, and order, are negatively correlated to impactful change. We've all been a part of a district initiative that didn't make the impact it was supposed to make because these four responsibilities weren't effectively realized. Introducing a new innovation, the study revealed, can cause team spirit, cooperation, common language, routine, and the level of staff member input to deteriorate.

Agency is a crucial part of education reform and change in the classroom, and also an important part of teachers feeling like their voice is making an impact. This study emphasizes the importance of being closely in tune with educators as we seek to make change, paying close attention to the four leadership responsibilities (culture, communication, input, and order).

Agency is illustrated often throughout the story of Oz. Dorothy gives voice and choice not only to her own interests, but also to those for whom she has grown to care. Her primary goal remains blindingly clear: to get home to her family, something she decides on her own. Most of her decisions as she travels along the yellow brick road are influenced by this goal. Even when she encounters problems, disappointments, and dangers, she persists with a high level of hope and agency. Remember, as a teacher, what your purpose is and the gifts you bring. No matter what is going on around you, this will always remain true.

Confidence

Though kind, considerate, and humble, Dorothy is no pushover. It is no coincidence that she meets and befriends three personalities who represent aspects she also doubts in herself. As she becomes more aware of her friends' differences (and, ultimately, their similarities), she is able to reflect on her own journey. The sum of their individual, though latent, strengths—wisdom, heart, and courage—inspires her to be more confident. This leads her to stand up for what she believes is right, and also to speak from the heart, with calmness, comfort, sincerity, and without any preconceived notions or hidden agendas.

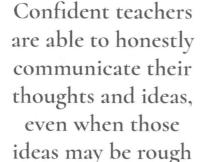

Confident teachers are able to honestly communicate their thoughts and ideas, even when those ideas may be rough or unproven.

Similarly, confident teachers are able to honestly communicate their thoughts and ideas, even when those ideas may be rough or unproven. How do you find this confidence? Well, you may be surprised to learn that you already have it. It is the intention you feel in yourself to do and spread good. This is not a dogmatic decree. It's simply accepting you alone are good enough, regardless of anyone else's opinions.

Drawing on Diverse Perspectives: Nathan's Experience

Sometimes, confident teachers can be perceived as rebels, mavericks, and overly independent.

As a school leader, I depended on the teachers perceived as rebels or mavericks to help me exemplify and inspire other educators to adopt new concepts, as well as to help encourage them to seriously question their own hesitations about change and growth. For example, I once worked with a teacher who seemed to pick out flaws or problems in every plan and initiative. Constantly questioning, always argumentative, and quite vocal at meetings, this teacher was quickly labeled by other colleagues as negative, but because of the confidence this teacher displayed, they maintained the status of being a well-respected voice in the school. I developed a relationship with the teacher and discovered that under the label of negativity lay wit, a healthy work ethic, and even a surprising positivity. Instead of going against the grain because they were jaded, this teacher was able to identify important weak spots that had otherwise gone unnoticed. The teacher was more than willing to scrutinize initiatives, down to the finest detail, and in the end make a strong contribution to the team. Once an idea went through this teacher's stringent assessment, other teachers had more confidence in the change I wanted to make and would champion it, so I had more confidence that divergent ideas would soar. The dissenters became the supporters of change. School leaders would be wise to depend on these nonconformists who understand the need for change and who are willing to change themselves. We all benefit when another pair of critical eyes evaluates our work, but we need to be confident enough to receive and integrate constructive criticism without fear of losing our identity or equilibrium.

When faced with a challenging scenario or new district initiative, remember the confidence that's already inside of you, that you can find by being true to yourself. As French philosopher, scientist, and mathematician René Descartes wrote in 1649:

> Those who are noble in this way are naturally inclined to do great things, and yet to undertake nothing of which they do not feel themselves capable. And because they value nothing more highly than doing good to other human beings, for the sake of which they regard their own interests as unimportant, they are always perfectly courteous, affable, and helpful toward one and all. Moreover, they are entirely in control of their passions: especially of desires, jealousy, and envy, since there is nothing the acquisition of which is not in their control that they think of sufficient value to warrant being greatly desired; and of hatred, since they esteem all human beings; and of terror, because they are fortified by confidence in their own virtue; and, finally, of anger, since, valuing, as they do, very little whatever is in the control of others, they never give their enemies the satisfaction of acknowledging that they are put out by such things.

Confidence isn't something you do, it's simply believing in yourself, your own integrity.

Cultivating Care

Clearly, one of Dorothy's strengths is her ability to nurture and care for those around her. Aunt Em modeled this well for Dorothy, who would have made Aunt Em proud as she exhibited graceful strength and care for her friends throughout their journey. As teachers, we have a tremendous responsibility to teach in innovative ways as our world quickly changes and to provide individualized learning opportunities so that each student can chart their personal growth. But one of the most—perhaps *the* most—important responsibilities we have as educators is to provide a nurturing and safe environment for kids to grow and thrive. This means that before we even plan lessons, create assessments, or consider instructional strategies, we are planning how to be the student's primary caretaker, from eight until three, Monday through Friday. Everyone needs to feel cared for in their own unique way.

The Gift of Caring: Herbie's Experience

I am an introvert. Sewn so completely into my genetic coding that even I would not be able to estimate its depths is the quiet contentment that can only exist in solitude, can only breathe in the space of serene peace and alone-time. Misunderstood by those who thrive in the sun, and social excess and distraction, mistaken for shy, I observe. Everything. I heard the whispered, shaded tone in the words you almost spoke. I noticed the microscopic tilt of your head as you pondered what you ultimately decided to not say. I effortlessly deciphered the truth behind the cacophony of words we both heard. I saw the way your eyes flickered over what you just saw, and I can tell you exactly what, why, and how you are now processing what you have just seen. I *could* tell you. But, of course, I will not, for your secrets are also my secrets. And, most likely, I have already flown back to the safety and quiet of home, wondering why I ever left my haven at all. Introverts live in midnight in broad daylight. We observe, and we are caretakers. Now, to be fair to my extroverted friends, caretakers of all kinds exist across the spectrum of all personality types, but my experience can only speak truth to the silent, serene solitude of the introvert.

Growing up in Santa Barbara, which basks in eternal sun along the southern coast of California (except for the summer months when, by some humorous twist of ironic chance, the city drowses in chilled, gray, clouded "June Gloom") my childhood was at once both idyllic and a nightmare. My mother was gentle, ever-laughing, kind yet fierce, protective, and with a hunger for knowledge and life that made all around her envious, while my father held the dubious role of abject villain. Belligerent, bigoted, and always like a lightning bolt of hate and anger, my father would literally lock me in my bedroom because he didn't want to see or hear me. He would even go so far as to take out all the lamps to further control the gay son he regularly said he didn't want (using other, more definitively descriptive language, the ugliness of which I will not honor by repeating here, but about which you can surely guess). Of course, there was an innate flaw to his plan to punish me, as there so often is with this type of bully. What he didn't know, was that I secretly loved being alone. His anger and vitriol existed almost like a distant planet light years away from mine. I would fill my days rearranging the furniture in my room, or voraciously reading the books in my library curled up in a down comforter. We are all products of our environments, and so it is no surprise that as I grew up as a very sensitive gay youth, the first person I decided I must take care of, and indeed rescue if possible, was my mother. I learned her moods, her modes of communication, her interests, what made her laugh, and what (just to be safe) subjects to avoid altogether.

We lived in a cozy California ranch home with a backyard filled with fruit trees and my mother's roses. One afternoon, when I was about four years old, I vividly remember taking a tumble as I went careening over our lawn trying to get back to my mother's waiting arms. Picking my little, confused self up off the grass, I was scared and started crying. My father was standing over us and I remember his face turning to a red fury of disgust and disappointment watching his son cry. He yelled at me, "Stop it, right now! Boys do not cry!" And with his declaration echoing through the trees, he turned and stalked back into the house. I knew that something was wrong, that there must be something wrong with me. I took a deep breath and started to bury my tears and fear. My mother, watching all of this, waited for my father to leave and then wisely turned to me and said gently, "If you are sad or scared, you go right ahead and cry, my love. It's ok to feel what you're feeling."

Well, of course, I looked at her, burst into tears and fell into her arms. I cried my four-year-old heart out until I forgot what I was crying about and we both started laughing. She taught me so very many things, but that day I learned gentleness. I learned to listen for the whispers in the face of a breaking storm. She taught me that true strength is born from a genuine care of others, especially those who cannot care for themselves. The gift of care does not come out of how much money you may or may not have, which car you drive, how loudly you yell, or how you can dominate others around you. It walks silently, with grace, all on its own throughout the world with open eyes, ears that listen, and with a heart that, though it may have been broken, remains courageous and open.

One of the most precious, long-lasting gifts you can give to your student is a listening ear, a shoulder to cry on, or a caring smile. Everyone has the capacity to care, and it starts with caring enough to get to know your students, what makes them laugh, smile, cry, and shout.

You Have Always Had the Power

Dropped into this strange and magical world, Dorothy is given a very powerful gift: the shoes of the Wicked Witch of the East. The exact nature and scale of the magic hidden deep within them remains secret and unknown. Ultimately, these shoes become her ticket home, but she doesn't realize this power until much later. You also have something very powerful, something that no one can take from you, but something that may yet remain hidden to you: your own powerful self-knowledge, which comes from your own unique perspective. When we are able to tap into this, we know exactly what we stand for. And when we sense that something is not right, we are able to self-correct. We find the practice of mindful meditation helps give your mind, body, and soul a space for self-discovery. There are many apps (Headspace, Calm, Peloton, etc.) and YouTube videos that have a plethora of meditation exercises. This practice allows you to experience emotions and thoughts as passing clouds, showing you that not every emotion or thought is worth reacting to. It helps you prioritize and use your energy and time wisely, allowing you to get a better sense of who you are. Journaling is also a helpful tool in gaining self-knowledge. It allows you to develop your thoughts, emotions, feelings, and values by extracting them from your subconscious.

Owning Your Power: Nathan's Experience

I always describe Herbie as my rock and the biggest support on my journey of self-actualization. Growing up, I had a deep yearning to discover who I was. Due to a combination of complicated environmental factors in my life at home as a young child, I developed a very negative perception of who I thought I was. I was supposed to be athletic, religious, overtly masculine, and to conform to the culture of the rural South. I had an interest in sports, but didn't feel particularly athletic and didn't care for fishing or hunting. I remember trying out for the basketball team and my father making fun of how I wasn't a very good dribbler. I was expected to adhere to Christian doctrine, which included being heterosexual. I did find that I was good at academics and so I put my energy into "being smart." I was taught, and told repeatedly, that if I did not conform to the expectations placed on me and become who everyone thought I *should* be that it was because something was wrong with me, because I was flawed. I learned as a small child that love was conditional upon being something I simply wasn't. For the longest time, I blamed others (the church and my father) for my negative self-view, but in actuality there were probably many forces at play that were hidden from my conscious awareness. As a gay teen, I did not have the support of my family or social circle. Neither did I have a positive role model to look up to. When I did share my stories with others, I was told that being myself was sinfully wrong—and I believed that. I was therefore left to try and find my way all alone.

When that happens, the stories we tell ourselves about who we are often end up being just that—stories, and if these stories have been built (either by us or by those around us) on foundations of prejudice and fear, they are nothing but lies and shadows. Through various experiences, I confidently became more aware of who I am and also saw that I wasn't truly being who I wanted to be. I started to see friends who were in similar situations make brave choices. Over time, I questioned more and more of the dogma I had accepted (and defended) all of my life, and started to develop a better sense of myself. I came to realize that I am not flawed.

Many times we let others tell us who we are. It's easier to imitate someone else than to be who we want to be. It's difficult to feel like the only one, all alone. So we remedy that by being what other people say we should be. This is the pattern that we must unravel.

Until I met Herbie, I had never had anyone affirm me like he did. He often said, and still repeats to this day, "You are perfect, just exactly as you are—you have no flaws." Like him, how gorgeous. A beautiful statement. You, too, are perfect. Do you believe that? If not, it may be a good time for some honest self-reflection. Though easier said than done, and probably a broader project than will fit into these pages, self-actualization is a process that will find you one way or another, if you are open to it happening. If we want to change and experience self-actualization, we must have an awareness of what we are. I have to remind myself daily of who I am and who I choose to be. Self-actualization takes continual effort and focus. Those of us who are fortunate enough to have friends, families, or Herbies in our lives to help light the way just happen to be a little bit luckier. Sure, there are times we find ourselves cranky or in a foul mood (we've all had those days where it takes all of the energy we can muster to walk through that classroom door), but maybe that's just an alert letting us know that something is off. And maybe it's time to stop, take a time-out, take as long as you need, and attend to the too-often-unaddressed priority of self-care. That's a very natural part of being human.

You Are the One You've Been Waiting For

Like Dorothy, you have always had the power all along. Your unique gifts, all the millions of incomparable, distinct qualities that make you one-of-a-kind, have been there since the beginning of your journey. No wicked witch can ever steal them from you. The worst thing the wicked witches of the world can ever do is to try and tell you lies about yourself so that you cannot see your own power.

Discovering that you've always had everything you ever needed can take a while. After all, it takes Dorothy traveling to a new world, journeying to the Emerald City, being kidnapped by winged monkeys, catching a quick nap in the deadly poppy field, making new friends, and learning powerful lessons from witches both good and wicked to find out that she could have returned home to Kansas just as soon as she arrived. When you are on your own journey of discovering this part of yourself, you might be tempted to craft a pseudo-personality that isn't really you but helps make navigating the unknown easier by "fitting in." That's not who you really are. Instead, figure out what shadow is hiding your soul and your core, remove it, and you'll see what was already there. Once you are able to embrace self-honesty, you will find you are more purposeful in your daily work of teaching and learning.

We've talked about Dorothy's kindness, agency, determination, and confidence. We've learned, along with her, that though we may sometimes doubt ourselves, thinking we're not smart enough, caring enough, or brave enough, we are in fact always enough just as we are. During her long trip through the many lands of Oz, Dorothy learns that love is central in her life. She chooses the gray Kansas prairie over the dazzling colors and wonders of Oz because she discovers just how much she loves Aunt Em. She both helps her friends, and accepts help from them, practicing the strength of reciprocal love. Again, we are reminded of our own journey. It isn't for glittering treasures or external recognition that we have been called to education. It is because we know, without a doubt, that it is who we are and what we are meant to do. It is one of the reasons we wake up in the morning: to support and provide a nurturing environment for students and—in their growth, development, and achievements—our own futures.

"Our little party of travellers awakened the next morning refreshed and full of hope . . . Behind them was the dark forest they had passed safely through, although they had suffered many discouragements; but before them was a lovely, sunny country that seemed to beckon them on to the Emerald City."

—L. Frank Baum,
The Wonderful Wizard of Oz

6

Collaboration: Journey in Oz

Dorothy and her teammates are able to achieve their goals because each has a sense of ownership in their shared success. Each character has their own reasons for journeying on the yellow brick road to see the Wizard, and Dorothy, the Scarecrow, the Lion, and the Tin Man all bring unique characteristics that are appreciated even when they do not see these qualities within themselves. It is the diversity of this team that helps to make them effective against the Wicked Witch. Successful collaboration occurs when we work together as a team to create ideas, and connect with others' intrinsic motivations.

Creating the Team

Whether we choose to believe it or not, we tend to favor interacting with teachers who are more similar to us in terms of thinking style, personality, perspectives, and opinions. Our differences can include more than background, race, gender, sexual orientation or identity, and so on. And even though people often feel more comfortable with others who are similar to them, like-mindedness hinders the exchange of different ideas and the intellectual processes that arise from disagreements—or even just different points of view. Generally, people prefer to spend time with people who are agreeable. Who doesn't enjoy having someone agree with you? Who doesn't enjoy being in the company of those who make you feel like you're doing and saying the right thing?

————— ❁ —————

Successful collaboration occurs when we work together as a team to create ideas, and connect with others' intrinsic motivations.

————— ❁ —————

But unchecked affirmation does not guarantee productivity and successful problem-solving. Being challenged takes deeper cognitive processing. It demands conflict resolution and emotional-energy expenditure. Through this cognitive struggle, new ideas emerge, and people learn from one another in unexpected ways and discover new solutions. Additionally, we have observed that the more we get to know someone whose perspective may differ, not only do we learn how much we actually have in common on a fundamental level, we also embrace the contrast of diverging viewpoints, if only subconsciously, and we find joy in the rewards of difference as our sphere of understanding and experience expands.

It's imperative for faculty to mirror the diversity of the community they serve. If diversity builds stronger collaborative thinking and innovation, why do schools have difficulty addressing diversity in working relationships? We would argue the answer to this question has to do with the fact that when emotions and dissenting opinions collide, the ability to act on decisions becomes more complex and time consuming as efficacy and patience erode. Additionally, because teachers are already strapped for time, it seems more efficient for them to sync up with the teacher/friend who will validate their opinion or teaching practice expediently and with no questions asked. Teachers find comfort in sharing with a colleague who shares or mirrors their beliefs.

However, when we choose to surround ourselves only with those who agree with us or who reinforce or validate our beliefs, we develop biases. Our willingness to examine and illuminate our own implicit biases is an important step in understanding the roots of injustice, discrimination, and racism in our country. We recommend reading *White Fragility* by Robin DiAngelo. This book will help show how white educators can crucially examine their own contributions to racism and help dismantle the system that perpetuates it. Every team needs diverse opinions and experiences. Look at the diversity in our team of friends on the yellow brick road. Even though their differences were quite stark, they found commonality in striving for the same goal—to safely reach the Emerald City—and leveraged each other's strengths along the way. It takes a team of people with diverse talents and skills, along with opportunities to communicate honestly and openly about challenges, for the team's shared vision to take shape. No matter how many winged monkeys, poison poppies, fighting trees, or shoe-stealing witches might want to join in the fun, a diverse team can capably stay the course.

How do you find these people with diverse talents and skills? Well, you have to seek out these original thinkers and recognize those who have outlandish ideas and are willing to contribute positively to the school culture. Befriend, connect with, hire, and promote people who create a culture of good and growth.

Ideation as a Team

The most innovative and successful educators are those who possess wide-ranging interests. You might think that their creativity comes from their vast and diverse knowledge. Creativity, after all, is the linking of ideas in ways that have never before been connected. Therefore, just possessing knowledge of something does not necessarily or automatically mean that creativity will follow, much less flourish. Open-mindedness and problem-solving skills can teach us to develop and use, to a better and higher purpose, the knowledge we already possess.

All of us, to some extent, borrow from others. In education we pride ourselves on repeating the mantra "There is nothing new under the sun." But the reality is that we are always seeking out something new. We hear about a new student engagement strategy. We see a powerful platitude posted on Twitter. We hear about a new app that's making waves in education. And we say, "I'm going to steal that for my classroom!" It's the culture of the PLN (professional learning network). Ideas are all around us, and often without realizing it, we incorporate these ideas or new terms into our everyday vocabulary. So much so that they quickly become educational jargon or buzzwords. This can have an unintended negative effect. What was once a wonderful idea with high potential has become an ambiguous acronym with nebulous meaning and lots of steps and processes.

Many of us jumped into the profession with the expectation that we were already supposed to know about RTI, MTSS, STEM, PBL, etc. We internalize this language, speak it, teach it, go through the motions in very individual ways. Borrowing ideas or being influenced by others' innovations is natural. But what's even more compelling—and what has the potential to transform the classroom—is *what we do with borrowed or influential ideas*. What matters is how deeply we assimilate them, make them ours, integrate them with our own experiences, thoughts, and feelings, and express them in a new way—our own way.

Constructive Collaboration:
Nathan's Experience

I once encountered a situation that propelled me to integrate an instructional practice into existing structures but make it work in a new way. When I was an administrator in a newly designated STEM school, based on economic and global trends, I knew we had to approach math and science instruction differently. Much of the nation had begun to shift to STEM programs and had started to adopt a kit-based, recipe-driven approach. Kits provide easy access to materials but often prove to be too prescriptive for students, with every student creating the same product/project and replicating the same procedure. If we are going to move toward more student inquiry and creativity, we must move toward more teacher inquiry and creativity as well. How do we create collaborative structures for teachers to co-create student-centric, problem-based challenges?

And that's where the shift occurred—from borrowing ideas to transforming them into tools that were more meaningful and more aligned to where we wanted to go as a team. My colleagues and I could have adopted the STEM status quo and simply asked students to create more projects. But our purpose for STEM was to provide opportunities to improve on iterations, solve local problems, choose technology tools that made sense, and apply mathematical practices to scientific (real-world) contexts. We realized students needed exposure to learning opportunities inside a "challenge-based" framework, solving problems through an inquiry-based approach, while applying engineering practices. So we began on this journey of creating STEM challenges as a medium for students to access integrated science and math content while utilizing an engineering design process to solve problems and deepen learning through important life skills.

Student learning through these rigorous and relevant challenges became the measure for mastery for learning. They developed aligned integrated lessons, performance tasks, and formative check-ins, and in the end, the challenges became indicators of learning. Students were now developing solutions for the overpopulation of deer in their community, testing their drinking water and proposing environmental solutions, and becoming directly involved in a building project for a new school, expressing their needs. Students were truly in the driver's seat of their own learning, solving local problems while building communication skills and expressing their most creative selves.

This new way of teaching and learning also meant we had to transform the way we planned. Planning for rigorous and relevant teaching and learning requires more than just the "common planning time." It represents a consistent, purposeful, and protected time where teachers immerse themselves in collaborative environments for the sole purpose of collectively creating integrated challenges and scaffolded lessons. Teachers' time is extremely valuable, and therefore we must ensure collaborative planning doesn't become another compliance-driven activity. Oftentimes, highly effective and passionate teachers jump in over their heads, with a disproportionate amount of actions/products being generated by those teachers. We developed professional learning opportunities for teachers to practice collaboration within newly developed elements like group norms, team roles, agreed-upon outcomes, and collective efficacy. These collaborative processes were automatically put into practice as teachers began to collaborate back in their respective buildings. Team leaders ensured weekly meetings were focused, and when they became unfocused, they circled back to agreed-upon norms—true collaboration. Accountability was naturally established around guiding practices (e.g., growth, excellence, transparency, etc.) that were displayed in meeting rooms.

As we dove into this transformational work, it prompted additional questions: As grade-level and whole-class challenges are developed, how do we address the differentiated needs of students? How do we address the different interests of students? When do students receive math instruction and practice with foundational skills? STEM projects/challenges had to fit in existing blocks of learning (e.g., a STEM block). We decided that learning blocks could and should be deconstructed and reconstructed. Teachers and administrators embraced flexibility in differentiation via small-group instruction during student-directed challenge time or planned to devote a block of time to teaching a mini-math lesson (e.g., determining ratios) while relating it back to the challenge's essential question, which had roots in science content (e.g., determining a solution for the overpopulation of deer). Differentiated student voice and choice promoted opportunities for students to choose their own pathways to a solution. If teachers spotted a deficit, they held an impromptu small-group or individual conversation inside this challenge-based environment.

The work above describes how we can incorporate new ideas as a team. We can discover or borrow an idea, but in doing so we can integrate it with our own collective experiences to make it better. Interestingly, when we have an idea, we tend to get overly attached to it, because it's ours. We must remember that our idea is only one of many different ways of generating solutions. We should ask ourselves why we like it and see if we can find reasons for rejecting it.

One final caveat with "new ideas": far too often, we develop PD or strategies that only consider two extremes in a continuum of intermediate possibilities. Either we do worksheets or projects, print or digital, traditional teaching or progressive. Not every concept has to be a dichotomy. The best way of meeting this dilemma is to evaluate new ideas (or initiatives or fads) critically, striving to maintain independence of mind, and avoid becoming too conventionalized in tradition. Considering a new idea can be a stimulus to thinking and can provide a new outlook on authenticity and creativity.

Connecting to the Motivations of Others

When working with others, we often focus on how to get them to see our perspectives. Although this is important, we must also remember to reciprocally, and sincerely, connect to others' experiences if we want to work together effectively. Experiences over time will contribute to the evolution of personal beliefs and attitudes. There are experiences that shape our motivations, which may not necessarily represent the beliefs themselves. For example, you may like to head to the gym to exercise because you want your heart to be healthy, while someone else likes to work out just as hard and as often as you because they desire a certain physique. The belief that the two of you hold that exercise is vital is the same, but the motivations that shape that belief are different. The same could be applied to teachers' preference for independent practice: the belief in independent practice is the same, but the worldview or motivation that shapes the belief might vary from teacher to teacher (be it in a teacher-facilitated environment, or as a part of homework).

Initiatives and change efforts often fail because the leaders focus too much on themselves and what appeals to them individually, and they assume teachers and students share their same value system. Many times, we, as education catalysts of change, ask, "How can we create buy-in?" or "How can we convince our fellow teachers to evolve?" If we are sincere about working together, we must approach the conversation differently. We should focus on how our actions connect to others' natural motivations. For example, some teachers feel they are likely to have more options and a greater sense of freedom, with respect to their specific values or worldviews, making them better able to choose one instructional strategy over another or embrace an innovative idea over a stagnant one. E.g., a district initiative is introduced, and some teachers feel as if the initiative is one more thing to do—one more plate to spin—on top of everything else. Other teachers may see the connection the initiative has to their current practice and adapt the new change into their own personal schema. As we understand the value of differentiated instruction because students learn in different ways, we must also apply the same understanding to the ways we learn as adults. We must focus on facilitating meaningful connections among teachers, students, instructional strategies, learning experiences, and tools to help create a cohesive learn-

If we are sincere about working together, we must approach the conversation differently. We should focus on how our actions connect to others' natural motivations.

ing environment. We can successfully make these connections when we understand how learners think, learn, and adapt to change. Change requires us to evolve, and therefore, we must create innovative ways to support teachers based on who they have become in the midst of changing circumstances.

Our friends on the yellow brick road had an innate sense of respect for each other. Some might argue that the strongest relationship in Oz, however, wasn't any of those fashioned in the magical land, but was instead the sweet, simple love of a girl for her little dog. Baum writes, "It was Toto that made Dorothy laugh, and saved her from growing as gray as her other surroundings. Toto was not gray; he was a little black dog, with long silky hair and small black eyes that twinkled merrily on either side of his funny, wee nose. Toto played all day long, and Dorothy played with him, and loved him dearly."

This relationship with Toto, in addition to the relationships Dorothy forged with her new friends, provided a level of comfort and security on her long journey back home. Collaborations, relationships, and ultimately classrooms must be founded in a similar trust, respect, and safety. There must be a backdrop of trust, security, and fun for any long lasting foundations to be laid successfully. Think about the best family gatherings around the dinner table, or just curling up next to your significant other in front of the TV. There is a sense of mutual respect, fun, and laughter. And that creates the safety to express a ridiculous idea for someone else to launch from. We must always be striving to create this same sense of safety as educators and leaders.

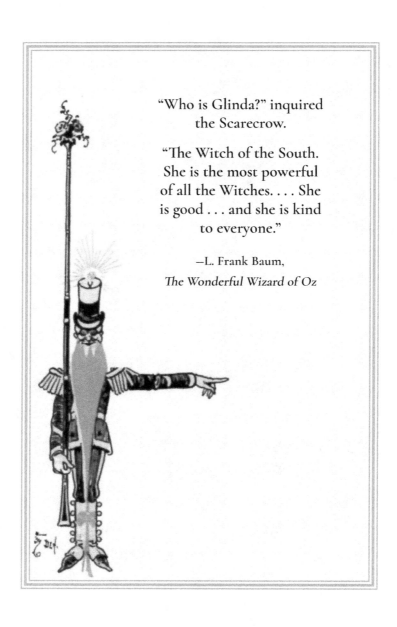

"Who is Glinda?" inquired
the Scarecrow.

"The Witch of the South.
She is the most powerful
of all the Witches. . . . She
is good . . . and she is kind
to everyone."

—L. Frank Baum,
The Wonderful Wizard of Oz

7

Leadership: Glinda

The Witch of the North tells Dorothy that the only way she will ever be able to return home to Kansas is to find the great and powerful Wizard of Oz and ask for his help. Upon the terrible discovery that the Wizard is in reality only a little humbug with no magical power at all, who has been living in fear of the wicked witches, hiding himself away behind the emerald walls of his city, refusing to be seen by anyone, he agrees to take Dorothy and Toto home in his hot air balloon. But just as Dorothy is at long last going to get her wish, Toto races off after a kitten and Dorothy must chase after him. The securing lines holding the balloon snap, and the Wizard floats away. What now?

Just when we think that all hope is lost and there is no way home, Glinda, the Good Witch of the South, reveals to Dorothy that her shoes can take her home! Where has this information been? Were all these adventures, new friends, and dangers just a distracting waste of time? Or did Dorothy have to endure a journey of self-discovery and learning before she could believe she possessed the power to return home? Just as the Scarecrow, the Tin Man, and the Lion needed to make their individual journeys to discover their wisdom, heart, and courage, Dorothy had a journey of her own to make before she would be ready to return home again.

Unbeknownst to her, Dorothy's journey gives her the sweeping and rare freedom to fully experience, reflect on, and endure the challenges leveled against her. That's truly the recipe for the most successful learning experiences: an opportunity for us to learn through discovery. And like Glinda, the best leaders give us this freedom—supporting, guiding, and cheering us on along the way.

This kind of freedom is needed for us to change the landscape of education. Education reform is often shrouded in overly complicated strategies and initiatives that don't provide us with the opportunity to independently evaluate those strategies and initiatives and judge them on their merits rather than their popularity. You'll hear educators say, "The school down the road has implemented this and it's working well." What does that mean, really? Every school and classroom is different, and we must evaluate all possible implications. For example, we might want to designate our school as a STEM school. But what are the hallmarks of a STEM school? What are the outcomes we are looking to accomplish? Citing case studies or examples of what other schools are doing, and making connections to educators' current reality can provide a powerful context for leading change. It allows us as teachers to accept the unpredictable nature of the world we live in, and we learn to adapt to this by taking risks and thinking in divergent ways. It's not the ideas themselves but the process of embodying a new way of thinking that can transform our practice.

However, as we move from theory to action (the theory that the yellow brick road can lead us home vs. actually putting in the work and walking down all those yellow bricks), we may struggle with jumping into the unknown due to the fears, pressures, and accountability measures that are placed on us. As leaders (principals, instructional coaches, teachers), how do we influence change in teacher practice while helping educators to own that positive change as theirs? We can lead effective change by establishing a culture of questioning, creating a structure for innovation, and giving teachers the freedom to influence grassroots changes instead of complying with top-down initiatives.

Ask Better Questions

Leaders can help teachers become successful and confident problem-solvers. In fact, it is imperative that they do. One of the most powerful forces for inspiring change in our daily lives is a simple tool that we all have: the ability to ask questions. Not only does this ability help us illuminate problems, but through a purposeful approach, our curiosity can help us create solutions, innovative ideas, and inspiration for new professional learning.

Let's explore a practical example of how questioning leads to better outcomes: the humble and ubiquitous button. Did you know buttons were not designed to function in the same way they do today? From their inception five thousand years ago, and for about three thousand years afterward, buttons were simply used to decorate clothing. It wasn't until the invention of the buttonhole that buttons became functional. It took society centuries to reimagine what the button could do. It took someone pushing back on the status quo and asking more questions, or perhaps a *better* question, about the *purpose* of a button and how we could use it for better applications. It all starts with a question. And we never know what outcome will result until we start with the simple ask. The most creative and successful educators tend to be the great question askers among us.

The act of answering a question with a counter-question is not that simple. Asking questions comes with the risk of being judged, ridiculed, and labeled. You might worry that the original asker of the question thinks you are deflecting because you don't know the answer. But isn't that okay—to not have all the answers? Earlier, we emphasized that it's the unanswered questions that make learning and life fun and intriguing. This kind of question asking must be modeled especially in leadership positions. Additionally, if you are continually asked questions, especially managerial questions—"What form do I use to lesson plan?" or "How can I get them to behave?"—you will want to consider the kind of culture that exists in the building. Ask yourself, "Am I developing a culture of shared values and open-ended inquiry or one of compliance and directive-given communication?" As leaders, we must partner with fellow teachers as change agents to ensure we create classrooms that cultivate innovation. There are a few strategies that can be used to encourage question asking, but it's more important that we first establish a culture of questioning, both in individual reflections and in a collaborative setting, so that we can provide the most in-depth exploration of the current reality and offer high-quality responses to what we'll do next.

Crafting Effective Questions: Nathan's Experience

When I was an administrator, I noticed that others sometimes began a coaching conversation with a teacher with the question "How do you think the lesson went?" Many times, teachers' responses would go one of two directions: "It went really well," or "It went well but could have gone better if I . . ." Even the most genuine and sincere responses to the aforementioned question didn't lead to the heart of the conversation that needed to happen.

When engaged in a conversation about a teacher's lesson, acknowledge the teacher's passion and your role in supporting them. Always begin with the why or purpose. Questions like these will keep the conversation focused on specific goals:

- "How did you tackle the problem we identified?"
- "Did you find our planning helpful in achieving the purpose?"

- "What evidence did you gather that shows students engaged in high-level thinking and learning?"

Another great conversation starter is "How did you reflect on the lesson?" This places the emphasis not on ability or perceived experience but on self-reflection for the sole purpose of growth. Additionally, this opens the door to conversations about metacognitive processes, inclusion of student feedback, and trusted peer observations.

It's easy to get stuck in a rut of feeling like the answer provider, especially when you're in a leadership role or viewed as an expert. Think about the leaders and mentors in your life that you most respected. There is a good chance they asked you questions you hadn't thought of, because they cared about helping you discover a better solution than the one you both already thought you had.

Creating a Structure That Works

School leaders often struggle to communicate a clear, common definition of what high-quality instruction really looks like in the classroom. They might have a picture of it in their minds, but articulating and giving concrete examples can be challenging unless we collaboratively develop common language and definitions around high-quality instruction. Teachers are justifiably skeptical about opening up their classrooms to others, especially when communication is unclear and vague. As a teacher, I welcomed feedback, but I also wanted to understand the practical value for me and for my students.

In education, we do not suffer from a deficit of tools, resources, and information. There is PD for nearly every topic and issue. Yet even with good PD, we often lack the internal structures, processes, and norms necessary to apply new learning knowledge and implement it successfully in classrooms. School leaders must develop a process and structure for translating all these ideas and strategies systematically into practice. Through this structure we can develop common language and a common agreement about instructional practice. By coming to terms with our instructional practice, we are able to ask better questions about our work as school leaders and determine what is happening or not happening in our schools. This process reveals weaknesses or blind spots in our thinking. For example, let's say that as a school community we have gathered data to suggest that teachers need support with creating meaningful learning experiences aligned to content standards.

Here are some questions we might ask that would eventually lead to better support for this instructional practice:

1. How do teachers know how to establish that learning experiences are aligned to established content standards?
2. What established content standards should be used?
3. If teachers know how to create tasks or learning experiences from content standards, how will we support them in doing so, and how will we monitor their work?
4. What does it mean to effectively create meaningful learning experiences?

Once school leaders establish a structure for collecting accurate schoolwide data (surveys, face-to-face meetings, classroom walk-throughs, etc.), they are then better able to facilitate collaborative discussions with teachers about the data and better support teachers in making tweaks in their instructional practices to ultimately promote deeper levels of student learning.

A word of advice, though: even with an agreed-upon structure for collecting data and talking about instructional practice, we must be very clear about indicators for effective practice. For example, if an indicator is "The teacher stated the learning target three times throughout the lesson," does this actually translate to a clear picture of what students believe they are working toward? A part of the problem is that we sometimes don't have a clear agreement on what these indicators actually look like in reality. Additionally, when the walkthrough is prioritized over the growing of our instructional practice, we tend to focus more on trying to get a check mark on the walkthrough form rather than really internalizing what that check mark means for the actual practice in the classrooms.

When developing walkthrough forms, we must do it in a way that allows teachers to provide ample input and ensure a narrower focus with clear and concise indicators. Additionally, walkthroughs shouldn't just be a principal- or coach-driven process. We must also create a consistent structure for teacher-to-teacher walkthroughs. For example, each teacher would establish their own goal for which they want feedback or support. (Example: How do we more effectively facilitate small groups? How can we improve student discourse?) The observer teacher would then conduct a brief—fifteen minutes—walkthrough, gathering evidence to provide suggestions for the host teacher on the stated focus, and then meet to review evidence and give feedback. Then the teacher pair would switch roles. Principals and even district administrators could provide classroom coverage for teachers while they engage in these walkthroughs with the results of the walkthroughs—now communally supported learning events—being shared across the faculty for increased efficacy and reach.

Invite Input

The Good Witch was able to reveal knowledge about how to finally get back home, but it was Dorothy who actually had to take the journey. In the education realms, leaders will take the journey with teachers, traveling through collaborative leadership, support, professional development, and providing resources. The days of corporate-style hierarchy in schools are gone (or at least they should be). We see principals modeling small-group instruction and teachers leading change in their schools. Teachers want to be treated as partners in the school vision and not just told how to teach and treated as replaceable and unimportant education tools. Teachers want to provide input, possess decision-making authority, and be a part of equitable leadership opportunities. And their roles, in the trenches, in real-time, make teachers uniquely positioned to offer invaluable observation and insight, if only they are granted the respect and latitude to realize their unique and individual identities.

Making input a valued cultural priority means more than just delegating tasks to the site-based leadership team, saying you have an "open-door policy," or sending a survey out to teachers before implementing new initiatives. Encouraging input should be a part of conversational DNA, allowing teachers to be fully engaged in and responsible for teaching and learning in the classroom. This starts with leaders not simply reacting to teacher questions and directives with the "right answer."

Listening and Learning: Nathan's Experience

As an administrator, I learned early on that I didn't have to have all the answers—because that is impossible. I also learned that the way I responded to questions sent a message about the fidelity of shared decision making, collaboration, and true openness to input. As I gained leadership experience, I developed a new mindset for listening to teacher concerns. When teachers approached me with questions, concerns, and issues, instead of knee-jerk reactions, I learned to guide the conversation in a way that allowed everyone to have input in a solution. (This also showed I was truly listening.) A leader's first response to a teacher should be an appreciation of the teacher sharing the concern: "Thank you for caring so much, and I hear you."

There are never enough hours in the day when you are a teacher, coach, or principal. You are often so busy that merely making the time to have a conversation about a concern or problem shows that there is a shared sense of problem-solving. The "I hear you" is also very important. Thanking someone for sharing a concern doesn't mean you agree with the premise of the concern or that you are going to provide a solution the teacher is proposing. You are simply acknowledging that you've listened carefully and objectively, and that you fully understand the concern. If this is not the case, there should be clarification before you move on in the conversation.

Because the concern has been shared with you as a leader, you now have the responsibility of deciding how it will be addressed. Not every concern will have an immediate next step. There might be others who now should also be involved or more information needed before a solution can be developed further. It's important for a leader to create a schedule of priority by saying, "I will follow through on your concern by . . ."

This shows that the leader is taking an active role in supporting the teacher, either by sharing next steps or exploring options for solutions together.

The last part of the conversation is crucial and is what gets left out far too many times: "Here is how you can help." The person coming to the leader with a concern often wants to be rid of any discomfort or negative implications surrounding the concern as soon as possible. This is understandable, but just sharing the concern doesn't eliminate any responsibility from the person sharing it. This last part of the conversation allows input to become a part of the problem-solving culture you are now leading in the building. Going a step further would allow for even more input: "How would you like to help with this?"

We opened this chapter with a reference to Glinda's leadership, but there is another leader who often gets overlooked: Dorothy. Young and lost in a new place, she was puzzled about how she would get out of Oz, if at all. And although she possessed limited knowledge about how she was going to get home and wasn't aware of the dangers she would face in this new and strange place, she was steadfast in her goal of getting back to Kansas. She stayed the course even when faced with adversity. She gained new friends in her journey and listened to their concerns and input. Her vision was clear and her approach was compelling enough to influence others to join her on the yellow brick road. Some leaders try hard to be something they are not, because of a perception they want to create about themselves. Dorothy was just herself: sincere, real, and vulnerable. And because of her genuine approach, she and all her friends grew during their journey on the yellow brick road in ways they could never have imagined.

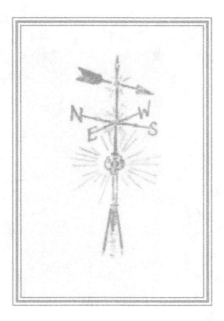

"I think you are a very bad man," said Dorothy.

"Oh, no, my dear; I'm really a very good man;
but I'm a very bad Wizard, I must admit."
—L. Frank Baum, *The Wonderful Wizard of Oz*

8

The Illusion of Education: The Wizard

At the end of the yellow brick road, the Wizard is revealed to be a fake. The only thing he is able to do for the four weary travelers is to act as a mirror for our friends. The Scarecrow only needed physical evidence of the wisdom he already possessed, the Lion was indeed already brave, the Tin Man wasn't heartless, and Dorothy found the defeat of the Wicked Witch was surprisingly easy— just add water. The true power of the Wizard, the only real gift he has to offer us, proves to be one of the most powerful and Oz-shattering of all: the revelation that perception and reality are often two very different things indeed.

When the alluring, dazzling magic of Oz begins to fade, it is revealed that the Wizard is only a "common man" born in Omaha, rather than an all-powerful wizard. Helpless little Dorothy can actually take care of herself and get herself back home to Kansas whenever she wants. Wickedness can be squashed or washed away with a little water and selflessness. Wisdom, heart, and courage are always there, if sometimes only hidden from view.

Further symbolizing the tug-of-war between perception and reality, the yellow brick road is revealed not to be the quintessential only solution, the gold standard, but simply another step along a road that may or may not be taken. Of course we are oversimplifying. To discredit all that was learned along the way would be to strip the charm and meaning from all of our stories. In the beginning, the magic shoes of the Wicked Witch of the East represented something of value, but whose power could not be fully realized until the end. The overarching theme of Oz is more of a transformation of consciousness, and about the power of self-awareness. In this final chapter, we'll focus on transforming our own perceptions of reality, in order to move the screen in the Wizard's throne room and to find out once and for all if there is indeed an all-powerful and elusive solution to our problems, or if we actually had all the answers within us all along.

There are many books and resources out there that tell teachers what perfect classrooms and perfect teaching should look like. These are perceptions crafted from a single world view, a single story. The inspiring writer Chimamanda Ngozi Adichie, in her powerful TED talk, stated, "The single story creates stereotypes, and the problem with stereotypes is not that they are untrue, but that they are incomplete. They make one story become the only story . . . I've always felt that it is impossible to engage properly with a place or a person without engaging with all of the stories of that place and that person. The consequence of the single story is this: It robs people of dignity. It makes our recognition of our equal humanity difficult. It emphasizes how we are different rather than how we are similar."

In this chapter, we are going to address the illusions of education and explore how to listen through the noise and truly open our eyes to reality.

The Illusion of Productivity and Support Tools

When seeking support, resources, and tools for the classroom, it's important to remember the most important resource: you. Your experiences. Your stories. Your strengths and talents. While we may think we need all these tools or resources, the truth is that we have what we need inside us. After years of enduring education plans and fixes, Nathan decided to develop his own personal teaching manifesto.

Nathan's Teaching Manifesto

1. Be fun and funny, smile, and laugh.

Smiles impact our interactions with others and our life experience as social beings. Smiles and laughter create an inviting tone, an essential warmth, and students learn best in these welcoming environments of understated inclusivity. Finding humor in the everyday is not only a tool for a more fulfilling life, but a powerful act of creativity as teachers and students. Those who find the "little joys" in life are the ones that smile often and laugh frequently. If you're having trouble finding the little joys, just look around and be present. Find a bird, a rock, or a tree, or simply take two minutes, walk away from your desk, and look up at the sky. There's always something somewhere that has the power to give us the gift of joy, if we are open and present to experience it. What that is, of course, varies from person to person. Herbie prefers dark, gloomy days when the fireplace is blazing and candles and warm blankets are everywhere, and I cannot be stopped if the sun is shining and the birds are singing.

Be aware of what's around you, and what resonates for you. It could be the smell of coffee in the morning, the crisp autumn air, a book you've been waiting to read, brunch with friends, or a quiet afternoon all to yourself. You will begin to find the nuances of the everyday. Gradually, and without even being conscious of it, you will start to notice the many small wonders surrounding you. From the wonders and subtle beauties of nature, to the neighborhood you live in, to that book you might be reading and can't wait to get back to, to the interactions you have each day, there are millions of experiences and details to dazzle and delight each of us, every single day. But do not fall into the trap of trying too hard to manufacture fun. Let go and see what happens. A quiet afternoon nap can be just as valuable as a weekend in Paris, and sometimes even more necessary.

2. *Create experiences, not activities.*

In my third year of teaching, I thought I'd found my groove. I had finally built up a repertoire of lessons and activities that students *seemed* engaged with. After all, I was a science teacher and thought I had the biggest opportunity to get students interested in learning. One day that bubble popped, when a student walked in and said, "This class is boring." I shared earlier how I responded. The student was right, and I needed to change the way I planned engaging instruction. I came to the conclusion that activities just aren't enough in the classroom. They don't stick with students, and they're not what's best for learning. Experiences, rather than activities, transform how students view the world and how they think about their own thinking.

3. *Be visibly invisible. It's about them, not you.*

During an instructional round one day, I heard about this phenomenal teacher I was going to visit at a school. I couldn't wait to observe their classroom. When I first walked into the classroom,

I couldn't find the teacher. It took me a few seconds of scanning until I spotted her. She was hunched over listening closely to a group of students having academic discourse about a math task they were working through. As I walked around the room, I noticed students piloting the conversation themselves. The teacher only guided from the periphery of the conversation. Her students defended and justified their answers to each other, with little prompting from the teacher. Her students believed that they were the leaders of the classroom and that they could help shape the thinking of other students. This was happening in supportive, collaborative ways: "I like the way you solved this problem." "I wonder if my answer would have been different if I had used your strategy." The teacher was visibly invisible in that the students knew she structured and planned the learning experiences but felt they were in charge of their own learning.

4. Treat every lesson as if you only get one chance.

Imagine that you're in your second, or forty-second, year of teaching and you're getting ready to teach a concept that you've already taught before. Or imagine it's Friday afternoon and you're ready to pack up for the weekend after a long and exhausting week. As you're planning for the next lesson or unit, the thought occurs: "Oh, I'll just recycle that lesson I've used before." It's easier and maybe more efficient to use what we've done before or in years past. Think about how you would feel in your role as a learner in a professional development session you're being asked to attend. What if the facilitator, speaker, or presenter used the exact same slide deck, activities, and strategies they'd used in the district in the next state, without any regard for your needs, the subject or grade you teach, or the school goals and norms you have in place. The same is true for those students in your class. Every group of students we have the pleasure, and honor, of teaching possesses different interests, backgrounds, experiences, and skill gaps, and therefore we must create experiences that connect to their intrinsic motivation. Yes, it's good practice to look at previous planning, but that should not be a starting point. Begin with the students in mind. What do they want to learn about, what do they need to know and be able to do in their ever-changing world, and how can you best support their individual needs? Then access your toolkit to see what tools will best accomplish this mission. Additionally, teaching a lesson as if it was your one and only chance increases your enthusiasm, energy, and urgency, so that every moment becomes an opportunity to make learning exciting and meaningful, as if it were your very first class, on your very first day of school, every day!

The Problem with Report Cards and Feedback

Teachers provide students with feedback in multiple ways, through grades, report cards, phone calls, and parent meetings at specific points throughout the year. The report card is a remnant of an archaic system that currently exists to communicate student achievement. This system cannot hope to accurately measure something as mercurial as true learning. Letter grades, grade point averages, and hundred-point system averages do not accurately represent a student's learning journey. Additionally, report cards only go out every six weeks at best, and students need highly specific, honest, and actionable feedback on a daily basis. Researchers Hattie and Yates have coined the phrase "empathy gap" to describe when teachers believe they're giving helpful feedback to the whole class, but students, when interviewed, say that this feedback is largely irrelevant to those who have mastered a learning target and often ignored by those who have not.

Praise is a common form of feedback, but this is often unhelpful because it fails to be constructive. (Think: "I like the way you're quietly walking down the hallway," or "You did a great job on your writing assignment.") This empty praise, although it may be well intentioned, shifts the students' attention to their own ability.

Effective feedback focuses on aspects of behaviors and learning outcomes, encouraging effort, motivation, perseverance, and communication. The specific or understandable nature of feedback ensures that students know exactly what parts of their reasoning need revisiting or what parts of their solution path contain inaccuracies. Actionable feedback ensures that students can take an objective view of teacher or student feedback and immediately make changes. Additionally, Hattie and Yates's research concludes that effective feedback can double the rate of learning and is among the top ten influences on achievement.

There are many ways that feedback can be incorporated into daily routines without taking the form of grades or report cards. Teacher-to-student feedback can be in verbal form in small-group settings or during station rotations. It can be in video form, through the use of video reflections. (I like to use WeVideo for this.) When students work in online documents, teachers can leave comments prompting students to rethink, reconsider, or reflect.

Putting the Student in the Driver's Seat: Herbie's Experience

Way back, in the mists of time—in high school—I had a chemistry teacher who was, shall we say, not overburdened with appreciation for me. I would be less than sincere here if I said my regard for him was not entirely reciprocal. In hindsight and fairness, I am sure I was his worst nightmare. Never completing my homework, showing up late to class—that is, if I decided to come back from lunch at all. (I mean, sixth-period chem class?! Come on . . .) In my defense, chemistry came easy to me, and this class was a complete bore. I breezed through writing and balancing all my chemical equations as if they were a second language, and if you had asked me then, I could have recited the periodic table of elements in my sleep. At the end of the semester, I scored an A– on the final without studying or preparing in any way. But because I had not turned in most of the homework assignments, the teacher failed me. Of course there was a parent-teacher meeting, and my mother was less than pleased, with both teacher and son. Even though I had learned the material, even though I had aced the final exam, because I hadn't met my teacher's conditional expectations, I received an F for the class. How is that fair?

Though he has taught me many things (most of which we'll leave for another time and a different book), I have learned from Nathan that research shows homework's only value resides in its ability to be meaningful, connected to students' interests, capable of reinforcing key concepts, and more comprehensive than simply asking students to memorize random facts to maintain information in working memory. (Author note: Nathan is actually dictating this last sentence from over my shoulder, but again, we'll save that for a different book.)

A few years later, in college, my English lit professor assigned *The Grapes of Wrath*. Never a fan of Steinbeck (which I quite happily remain, thank you), I approached the professor with my misery and, during our meeting, mentioned I had recently begun reading Tolstoy's *Anna Karenina*. After his surprise at learning one of his students was reading a classic of his own accord had subsided, he complimented my choice and made a very generous offer to me. If I agreed to adhere to his class's reading schedule for having the book completed, he would accept my reading Tolstoy instead. He offered to design a final exam specifically for me based on the tragic train-traveling temptress so that I would be spared the horror and tedium of Steinbeck. Well . . . I couldn't believe my good luck and thanked him for his kindness. (Though of course in the back of my mind I couldn't help but wonder if I'd just jumped right in front of Madame Karenin's train myself: Tolstoy's 800+ pages would take decidedly longer to get through than Johnny S.'s mere

400.) The semester passed quickly and, because I was so consumed with Vronsky and Anna, so too did those 800 pages. True to his word, while my classmates found themselves espousing the agrarian wonders (yawn) of Steinbeck, I sat down to the final my professor had kindly crafted just for me. I vividly, and proudly, remember scoring a 91. Thus saved from the dreaded dust bowl drama, my life continued along on its merry way. I have never forgotten the care and genuine interest I felt from my professor and his class. I had been given the rare gift of learning for its own sake, independent of ego or obsolete curriculum.

Exposing Our Perceptions

Earlier, we explored how leaders must create a clear structure of classroom observations and feedback. Additionally, we must redefine and clarify our role as educators. Teaching is too often perceived as a low-skill profession, and many times as educators we may inadvertently reinforce this perception. There are many political and societal perceptions about what our responsibilities are in the classroom and the expectations that teachers are held to. When we clarify our role and the guiding principles that shape our work, we can be confident that our work is in direct positive correlation to student outcomes.

Perceptions about the success of a school are unfortunately still measured by, and mired in, antiquated benchmarks like test scores. When schools are met with these results, the school community immediately begins to consider why it is their students are receiving low scores. Leadership may come to the conclusion that a newly designed assessment is necessary to explain the low scores and that students weren't adequately prepared for the assessment because they were only exposed to low-level tasks. Or school leaders may conclude that a lack of fidelity to a consistent and sound instructional framework explains the results. These conclusions begin to affect the perceptions of everyone in the school community. With the school leaders' paradigm now shifted, and with this new narrative in place, they tell themselves they could have, and perhaps should have, anticipated lower test scores. The leaders may react and build an action plan to address the low test scores.

In this scenario, leadership focused on the event itself and its consequences. As educators, we've come to understand the problem with forming hard-and-fast conclusions based on assessment results. Unfortunately, the perceptions we form don't always align with reality. We may later come to the conclusion that the test items actually were not well designed or that they did not closely relate to innovative real-world classroom practices. The point is that we begin to see the fragility of our perceptions and acknowledge that we may create binders full of action plans, force new PD on teachers, or change our vision, only to have it changed again when another unexpected event occurs. These changing perceptions lead us to conclude that it's not the ideas themselves but rather the process of adopting a new type of thinking, and awareness of how our minds react, adapt, accept, or resist change that may finally transform our practice.

> As educators, we've come to understand the problem with forming hard-and-fast conclusions based on assessment results. Unfortunately, the perceptions we form don't always align with reality.

There is a myriad of assumptions operating in our daily lives, governing our actions. Most of our perceptions about high-level teaching practice are not typically grounded in strong descriptive language. We'll say: "If teachers are given a sound curriculum, then students will have access to higher levels of learning."

Here's an example of the overarching assumptions we make that drive our subjective behaviors, in the area of bettering health. My assumption: When I drink peppermint tea at bedtime, I will sleep better and longer. My strategy is now to always drink tea before bed, because sipping hot tea equals better sleep. My experience: This is testable, and it turns out that it is not always accurate. I drank tea the other night before bedtime, and I got awful sleep. There were obviously other factors going on. Was it the wind howling outside waking me up? Was I more stressed than normal? Did I have dinner too late? We base our assumptions and perceptions on past experiences. I might start drinking tea earlier or change to a new kind of tea until I get the results I want. (Herbie suggests a nightcap instead, and it works for him. Just saying.) Based on those results, I'll start to shift my perceptions, and this is typical of human behavior.

What can be concerning is that we base perceptions and sweeping behavior on outdated evidence because we feel more comfortable doing what we've always done, even though it may include an outdated mindset. There's a reason they're called "comfort zones." It's not always comfortable to shift our actions to match new evidence. It's the reason that lecturing to endless rows of desks remains the mode, and teacher-centric classrooms are still popular—because it's easier and more comfortable to be in control and to teach in a way that's been done for decades. Exposing this gap between evidence for change and our current behaviors is crucial. We must uncover our perceptions if we are going to successfully reflect on our practice and see reality all around us. Most of our assumptions remain subconscious until we start to intentionally and explicitly name and decide how these assumptions affect our behavior.

Healthy Skepticism

Once we've reflected on our practice (evaluated our perceptions and our current behaviors), we must equip ourselves with an open mind but balance it with healthy skepticism. Healthy skepticism keeps us aware of potential deception and manipulation. In the case of our friends in Oz, one could be a bit skeptical about a few of the events in the original book. Is the Wicked Witch really dead because Dorothy threw a bucket of water at her? Surely she will reappear somewhere else, as typically happens with villains of this scale. But alas, she really is dead. But the direct result of discovering that the Wizard has been misleading us all along suggests that a healthy sense of skepticism can sometimes be wise. It compels the reader to reevaluate the trust placed in the narrative.

Philosopher Carl Sagan developed a Baloney Detection Kit as a tool to help detect deception. The kit advocates healthy skepticism, not only in education, but in everyday life. Sagan shares these nine tips:

1. Wherever possible there must be independent confirmation of the "facts."
2. Encourage substantive debate on the evidence by knowledgeable proponents of all points of view.
3. Arguments from authority carry little weight—"authorities" have made mistakes in the past. They will do so again in the future. Perhaps a better way to say it is that in science there are no authorities; at most, there are experts.
4. Spin more than one hypothesis. If there's something to be explained, think of all the different ways in which it could be explained. Then think of tests by which you might systematically disprove each of the alternatives. What survives, the hypothesis that resists disproof in this Darwinian selection among "multiple working hypotheses," has a much better chance of being the right answer than if you had simply run with the first idea that caught your fancy.
5. Try not to get overly attached to a hypothesis just because it's yours. It's only a way station in the pursuit of knowledge. Ask yourself why you like the idea. Compare it fairly with the alternatives. See if you can find reasons for rejecting it. If you don't, others will.

6. Quantify. If whatever it is you're explaining has some measure, some numerical quantity attached to it, you'll be much better able to discriminate among competing hypotheses. What is vague and qualitative is open to many explanations. Of course there are truths to be sought in the many qualitative issues we are obliged to confront, but finding them is more challenging.

7. If there's a chain of argument, every link in the chain must work (including the premise)—not just most of them.

8. Occam's Razor. This convenient rule-of-thumb urges us when faced with two hypotheses that explain the data equally well to choose the simpler.

9. Always ask whether the hypothesis can be, at least in principle, falsified. Propositions that are untestable, unfalsifiable are not worth much. You must be able to check assertions out. Inveterate skeptics must be given the chance to follow your reasoning, to duplicate your experiments and see if they get the same result.

A couple of examples in education that could be put to the test using principles from Sagan's Baloney Kit are learning styles research and cognitive research theory. Previous research has shown that students learn better when teaching is tailored to their specific learning styles. The latest research has yet to confirm this conclusion, and it's now widely accepted that all students should benefit from learning through various methods. Regarding cognitive theory, many took Bloom's hierarchy of learning to mean that we must always focus on the basics before we move on to more complex thinking. But Bloom never said students must always "know the basics" before engaging in higher-order thinking. The assumption that students have to memorize factual knowledge before they can think critically will keep them from fully experiencing meaningful learning.

The Illusion of Student Achievement and ADHD

There is an illusion that has plagued teachers for the past few decades. It's the illusion of student achievement scores measured by standardized tests. For as long as standardized testing has reigned as a means for accountability, these underlying (or overt) assumptions have existed based on how we measure teacher effectiveness:

- Reading and math scores are not where they should be.
- There is a crisis in our education system.
- Test scores will go up if we teach better.
- Test scores will go up if we use a research-proven program.

Here is the truth—time and time again, studies have shown that test scores are highly correlated with socio-economic conditions that exist for the student. It's been concluded that 60 percent or higher of achievement scores are correlated to out-of-school factors.

The struggle associated with learning (solving math problems and decoding words) is, in fact, quite normal, and a long, chaotic, and complex process. Teaching is very complex and is unique to the worldview of the teacher and to the individual needs of each child. There is no certifiably "best" method for teaching children who experience difficulty with learning math concepts or how to read.

Education researcher Sir Ken Robinson (2010) shares his view in a TED talk about the modern epidemic of ADHD. The truth is that it's not an epidemic. Our students today are frequently being medicated as routinely as certain styles fall in and out of season.

He goes on to say that our children are living in the most intensively stimulating period in the history of the earth. They are bombarded daily with media, apps, video games, and social media from multiple access points: computers, TV, tablets, watches, and iPhones. When they come to school, we get upset that they think our classroom is boring and we give them consequences or a diagnosis because they are easily distracted.

Sir Robinson correlates the existence of ADHD to the rise of the standardized testing emphasis. Students are given drugs to get them focused and calmed. Our classrooms should be spaces of beauty, creativity, excitement, and discovery. How are students expected to fully experience learning if 1.) they aren't being taught in a way that reinforces meaning, 2.) we are continually industrializing education by forcing students to memorize, conform with school initiatives, and comply with rules, and organizing them into standardized structure, and 3.) we are giving them drugs that weaken the senses.

The way we teach must not be measured by inaccurate standardized test results that are not correlated to students' living conditions. It also must not be framed as some magic fix. Demands that all children attain some prescribed proficiency in a subject and by a certain grade level are arbitrary, artificial, and unnatural.

Instead of telling students all the things they will or should learn each day, we should inspire them to seek out opportunities to see the wonder in the everyday things, discovering the joy in learning. True learning isn't rushed and is characterized by temporary bewilderment and confusion, followed by curiosity and comprehension. The way we teach should always be guided by how our students learn. Teaching students how to think goes beyond knowledge wheels, higher-order-thinking triangles, and verbs in a state standard. It really means learning how to actively construct—and distill—meaning from experience, and to fully exercise an individualized expression of themselves.

EPILOGUE

At the end of the book, we get the homecoming we've been longing for. Aunt Em, coming out of the house to water her cabbages, sees Dorothy and "folds the little girl in her arms and covers her face with kisses." Faced with the glittering wonders and treasures of Oz, as different from the stark gray prairie as it is possible to be, Dorothy realizes just how important and utterly irreplaceable her home really is. It required her losing sight of it for a little while for her to discover both what she already had, and her now deeper appreciation of it. Sometimes we find the most when we are lost. We hope you've discovered more of yourself throughout the journey of this book and that you have come to a place, whether for the first time, or by way of coming "home" again, of recognizing the strength and uniqueness that you, and only you, possess.

That brings us back to Nietzsche's wise words about the bridge. No program, tool, or PD can carry you across a bridge that leads you in a direction that's not true to who you are. It's tempting to go on some kind of existential awakening tour to find out who you really are—to go on some soul-searching mission to gain new courage, intelligence, spirit, and heart. But if you stop pursuing answers beyond yourself and listen, your true heart's desires and a deep sense of self will make themselves heard.

———— ❁ ————

If you stop pursuing answers beyond yourself and listen, your true heart's desires and a deep sense of self will make themselves heard.

———— ❁ ————

When we moved to Maine, we kept hearing about black bears. It was fascinating to think we might stumble upon one while taking a walk through our woods. A couple months of winter passed, and we didn't see a single black bear, not even a moose. And then one cold winter night, around two a.m., we found him, or rather *he* found *us*. One of our security cameras caught him casually walking up to and looking through our front door! He sniffed around a bit, found our bird feeder, climbed up a column on the front porch to get a good snack, and then moved on. (We named him "RoBEARto" by the way.) The very next year on the anniversary of his first visit, he came to visit again, this time just sniffing the porch and walking away. The soul (or spirit, or however you identify your core) is like that black bear. We didn't discover him by tromping through the woods yelling, "Mr. Bear, Mr. Bear, come out, come out wherever you are!" He, like most bears, is clever and independent, knows what he wants, yet is also reserved and sometimes hidden only just out of sight. Just as the stillness of a cold winter's night coaxed the bear to our doorstep, we can best find ourselves in stillness and in the comfort of trusting and positive environments.

One final note: teaching has been referred to as "a calling." We look at it a bit differently. Teaching is a gift. It's not some prize to be achieved or some profession to find success in, but a gift to be completely realized, nurtured, and protected. That gift, that spark, is already there; this is the true self you must realize. No professional development session, strategy, or tool can help you discover it. Only you can decide that you will be the person you were born to be. Once that happens, you will find a wellspring of wisdom, heart, courage, and spirit, just like our friends did in Oz. You will find that you are enough, exactly as you are. And you will find that you are home at last.

REFERENCES

Adichie, Chimamanda Ngozi. "The Danger of a Single Story." TED Talk. http://www.ted.com/talks/chimamanda_ngozi_adichie _the_danger_of_a_single_story?language=en.

Bernstein, Ethan. "Collaborate, but Only Intermittently, Says New Study." *Harvard Business Review* (August 13, 2018). https://www. eurekalert.org/pub_releases/2018-08/hbs-cbo081018.php.

Cameron, Greg, and Tim Waters. "The Balanced Leadership Framework." *McRel* (2007). https://files.eric.ed.gov/fulltext /ED544245.pdf.

Descartes, René. *The Passions of the Soul.* 1649.

Dewey, John. *Art as Experience.* New York: Minton, Balch & Company, 1934.

Dewey, John. *How We Think.* Boston: D.C. Heath and Company, 1910.

Holiday, Ryan. *Ego Is the Enemy.* London: Profile Books Ltd., 2016.

Nietzsche, Friedrich. *Schopenhauer as Educator*, Chicago: Regenery, 1965.

Robinson, Ken. "Changing Education Paradigms." TED Talk, 2010. www.ted.com/talks/sir_ken_robinson_changing _education_paradigms.

Sagan, Carl. *The Demon-Haunted World: Science as a Candle in the Dark.* New York: Random House, 1996.

ACKNOWLEDGMENTS

From Nathan:

Thank you to Dave and Shelley Burgess, and to the DBC staff for their tremendous support. Dave and Shelley believed in us and in the idea of this book from the beginning. The fact that I have never seen an education book written by a husband couple until now speaks volumes about who you are as humans, and your mission for equality and learning for all.

The utmost gratitude to my best friend, co-author, and brilliant mind, my husband, Herbie. The inspiration and conception of this book was yours. This book would have not been possible without your unconditional love, unending support, and the sincerest of affirmation, to help me believe in myself enough to have the courage to open up about my journey. Getting to spend my days with you is pure magic and immeasurably blissful. Thank you. I love you very much.

My professional mission is to help all kids feel valued and to see the amazing gifts they possess so that they may be their most creative selves. Clayton and Anna, my own children, thank you for the example you set for the world. Clayton, thank you for your courage to be yourself and stand up for what you believe in, and Anna, thank you for your heart for humankind and the happiness you spread daily.

And finally, thank *you*—yes, I'm talking to you—for going on this journey with us and for your support in helping all children grow and thrive.

From Herbie:

Thank you to all the teachers I have met along the way, both professional educators and also all those "unintentional teachers" working double-duty wearing the mantles of family, friends, and colleagues. Whether it was your intention to teach me something, or if it happened simply all by itself, or entirely by accident, your lessons and gifts have left indelible marks on my life, making it richer, larger, and more layered than it could ever have been had I never left "home" to find it.

To Dave and Shelley, and to everyone who helped our book along our own little winding section of the yellow brick road: Thank you for your belief in us, your guidance, and for accepting us into your warm and generous family.

To my favorite teacher, my best friend and husband, Nathan: Your unending, depthless love, good humor, infectious laugh, brilliant mind, playful, inexhaustible spirit, and infinite patience is more precious to me than words can ever express. I am somehow prouder of you every moment. And, sorry I'm not sorry, I will continue to bring up your accomplishments and phenomenal work to complete strangers at every opportunity. (It would take an entirely different book to even attempt to convey how much I love you.) You teach me something new every single day about the world, and have set me free to be able to discover it for myself with a brand-new set of eyes. You single-handedly moved our little family across the country, and now, everyone at Grayskull—Kevs, SBJ, Rock, Blaze, Dasher, and Yah—face nothing but endless days of new adventures and discoveries . . . and bread pudding and mimosas.

To my very first teacher, my mother: I miss you every single day. Among all the innumerable gifts you gave to me, you bestowed upon me your own love of learning, of reading, of storytelling, of mystery and magic. We first watched *The Wizard of Oz* together before I was even old enough to sit up by myself, and so you piled cushions around me to keep me upright, sitting beside me and enjoying every moment. Every year, when it was on TV (a day that was rivaled in scale and scope only by Christmas), we would watch it together. You took my hand and walked me through the realms of Oz, Wonderland, Neverland, Toad Hall, and Lyonesse, and introduced me to new friends like King Birtram, the White Rabbit, Hercule Poirot, Miss Jane Marple, Winnowill, the Hobbits, the Cheysuli, and the elves of Shannara, who would comfort me and keep me company in those long dark days after you had to leave me. Your legacy of learning something new every day is something I carry in my pocket to this day. I will always "love you more than anything." I hope I make you proud . . .

ABOUT THE AUTHORS

Dr. Nathan D. Lang-Raad is an international speaker, author, and professional learning facilitator. He is the Chief Education Officer at WeVideo. Throughout his career, he has served as a teacher, principal, university adjunct professor, consultant, and education strategist. He was director of elementary curriculum and instruction for Metropolitan Nashville Public Schools, as well as the education supervisor at NASA's Johnson Space Center. He is the cofounder of the Bammy Award–nominated #LeadUpChat, an educational leadership professional learning network (PLN) on Twitter. He serves on the boards of the Student Voice Foundation, Rocket Ready EDU, and the ISTE EdLeaders PLN. Nathan is the author of *Everyday Instructional Coaching* and *WeVideo Every Day*, and is co-author of a book with Dr. Robert J. Marzano, *The New Art and Science of Teaching Mathematics*. Nathan resides in the beautiful state of Maine with his husband Herbie. To learn more about Nathan's work, visit drlangraad.com or follow him on Twitter and Instagram: @drlangraad.

Herbie Raad was born and raised in Santa Barbara, California. Throughout his career as a professional singer, he has been privileged enough to have performed all over the world. Hard at work on his first full-length novel, Herbie resides in the beautiful state of Maine with his husband, Nathan, and their three Siamese children: Kevin, Rock, and James. To learn more about Herbie and his work, visit herbieraad.com and follow him on Twitter and Instagram: @herbieraad.

MORE FROM
Dave Burgess Consulting, Inc.

Since 2012, DBCI has been publishing books that inspire and equip educators to be their best. For more information on our titles or to purchase bulk orders for your school, district, or book study, visit **DaveBurgessConsulting.com/DBCIbooks**.

More Inspiration, Professional Growth & Personal Development

Be REAL by Tara Martin

Be the One for Kids by Ryan Sheehy

The Coach ADVenture by Amy Illingworth

Creatively Productive by Lisa Johnson

Educational Eye Exam by Alicia Ray

The EduNinja Mindset by Jennifer Burdis

Empower Our Girls by Lynmara Colón and Adam Welcome

Finding Lifelines by Andrew Grieve and Andrew Sharos

The Four O'Clock Faculty by Rich Czyz

How Much Water Do We Have? by Pete and Kris Nunweiler

If the Dance Floor is Empty, Change the Song by Dr. Joe Clark

P Is for Pirate by Dave and Shelley Burgess

A Passion for Kindness by Tamara Letter

The Path to Serendipity by Allyson Apsey

Sanctuaries by Dan Tricarico

The SECRET SAUCE by Rich Czyz

Shattering the Perfect Teacher Myth by Aaron Hogan

Stories from Webb by Todd Nesloney

Talk to Me by Kim Bearden

Teach Better by Chad Ostrowski, Tiffany Ott, Rae Hughart, and Jeff Gargas

Teach Me, Teacher by Jacob Chastain

Teach, Play, Learn! by Adam Peterson

TeamMakers by Laura Robb and Evan Robb

Through the Lens of Serendipity by Allyson Apsey

The Zen Teacher by Dan Tricarico

Like a PIRATE™ Series

Teach Like a PIRATE by Dave Burgess

eXPlore Like a Pirate by Michael Matera

Learn Like a Pirate by Paul Solarz

Play Like a Pirate by Quinn Rollins

Run Like a Pirate by Adam Welcome

Tech Like a PIRATE by Matt Miller

Lead Like a PIRATE™ Series

Lead Like a PIRATE by Shelley Burgess and Beth Houf

Balance Like a Pirate by Jessica Cabeen, Jessica Johnson, and Sarah Johnson

Lead beyond Your Title by Nili Bartley

Lead with Appreciation by Amber Teamann and Melinda Miller

Lead with Culture by Jay Billy

Lead with Instructional Rounds by Vicki Wilson

Lead with Literacy by Mandy Ellis

Leadership & School Culture

Culturize by Jimmy Casas

Escaping the School Leader's Dunk Tank by Rebecca Coda and Rick Jetter

From Teacher to Leader by Starr Sackstein

The Innovator's Mindset by George Couros
It's OK to Say "They" by Christy Whittlesey
Kids Deserve It! by Todd Nesloney and Adam Welcome
Live Your Excellence by Jimmy Casas
Let Them Speak by Rebecca Coda and Rick Jetter
The Limitless School by Abe Hege and Adam Dovico
Next-Level Teaching by Jonathan Alsheimer
The Pepper Effect by Sean Gaillard
The Principled Principal by Jeffrey Zoul and Anthony McConnell
Relentless by Hamish Brewer
The Secret Solution by Todd Whitaker, Sam Miller, and
  Ryan Donlan
Start. Right. Now. by Todd Whitaker, Jeffrey Zoul, and
  Jimmy Casas
Stop. Right. Now. by Jimmy Casas and Jeffrey Zoul
Teach Your Class Off by CJ Reynolds
They Call Me "Mr. De" by Frank DeAngelis
Unmapped Potential by Julie Hasson and Missy Lennard
Word Shift by Joy Kirr
Your School Rocks by Ryan McLane and Eric Lowe

Technology & Tools

50 Things You Can Do with Google Classroom by Alice Keeler
  and Libbi Miller
50 Things to Go Further with Google Classroom by Alice Keeler
  and Libbi Miller
140 Twitter Tips for Educators by Brad Currie, Billy Krakower,
  and Scott Rocco
Block Breaker by Brian Aspinall
Code Breaker by Brian Aspinall
Control Alt Achieve by Eric Curts
Google Apps for Littles by Christine Pinto and Alice Keeler

Master the Media by Julie Smith

Reality Bytes by Christine Lion-Bailey, Jesse Lubinsky, and
Micah Shippee, PhD

Sail the 7 Cs with Microsoft Education by Becky Keene
and Kathi Kersznowski

Shake Up Learning by Kasey Bell

Social LEADia by Jennifer Casa-Todd

Stepping up to Google Classroom by Alice Keeler and
Kimberly Mattina

Teaching Math with Google Apps by Alice Keeler and
Diana Herrington

Teachingland by Amanda Fox and Mary Ellen Weeks

Teaching Methods & Materials

All 4s and 5s by Andrew Sharos

Boredom Busters by Katie Powell

The Classroom Chef by John Stevens and Matt Vaudrey

The Collaborative Classroom by Trevor Muir

Copyrighteous by Diana Gill

Ditch That Homework by Matt Miller and Alice Keeler

Ditch That Textbook by Matt Miller

Don't Ditch That Tech by Matt Miller, Nate Ridgway, and
Angelia Ridgway

EDrenaline Rush by John Meehan

Educated by Design by Michael Cohen, The Tech Rabbi

The EduProtocol Field Guide by Marlena Hebern and Jon Corippo

The EduProtocol Field Guide: Book 2 by Marlena Hebern and
Jon Corippo

Instant Relevance by Denis Sheeran

LAUNCH by John Spencer and A. J. Juliani

Make Learning MAGICAL by Tisha Richmond

Pure Genius by Don Wettrick

The Revolution by Darren Ellwein and Derek McCoy
Shift This! by Joy Kirr
Skyrocket Your Teacher Coaching by Michael Cary Sonbert
Spark Learning by Ramsey Musallam
Sparks in the Dark by Travis Crowder and Todd Nesloney
Table Talk Math by John Stevens
The Wild Card by Hope and Wade King
The Writing on the Classroom Wall by Steve Wyborney

Children's Books

Beyond Us by Aaron Polansky
Cannonball In by Tara Martin
Dolphins in Trees by Aaron Polansky
I Want to Be a Lot by Ashley Savage
The Princes of Serendip by Allyson Apsey
The Wild Card Kids by Hope and Wade King
Zom-Be a Design Thinker by Amanda Fox